THE EVERYTHING KIDS' Baseball Book

8TH EDITION

From baseball's history to today's favorite players—
with lots of home run fun in between!

Greg Jacobs
Reporter/Statistician, STATS, LLC

and

Joe Gergen
Sports Reporter

A adamsmedia
Avon, Massachusetts

PUBLISHER Karen Cooper

MANAGING EDITOR, EVERYTHING® SERIES Lisa Laing

COPY CHIEF Casey Ebert

ASSISTANT PRODUCTION EDITOR Alex Guarco

ACQUISITIONS EDITOR Pam Wissman

DEVELOPMENT EDITOR Brett Palana-Shanahan

EVERYTHING® SERIES COVER DESIGNER Erin Alexander

An Everything® Series Book.
Everything® and everything.com® are registered trademarks of F+W Media, Inc.

Published by Adams Media, a division of F+W Media, Inc.
57 Littlefield Street, Avon, MA 02322. U.S.A.
www.adamsmedia.com

ISBN 10: 1-4405-7176-7
ISBN 13: 978-1-4405-7176-3
eISBN 10: 1-4405-7177-5
eISBN 13: 978-1-4405-7177-0

Printed by RR Donnelley, Harrisonburg, VA, U.S.A.

10 9 8 7 6 5 4 3

July 2015

Many of the designations used by manufacturers and sellers to distinguish their products are
claimed as trademarks. Where those designations appear in this book and F+W Media was
aware of a trademark claim, the designations have been printed with initial capital letters.

Interior illustrations by Kurt Dolber.
Puzzles by Beth L. Blair.
Cover images © 123rf.com.

This book is available at quantity discounts for bulk purchases.
For information, please call 1-800-289-0963.

Visit the entire Everything® series at *www.everything.com*

Contents

To Milo Cebu,
who attended his first
Cardinals game this year,
and brought them luck.

I would like to thank my wife
and sidekick, Burrito Girl, who
puts up with me when I write
about sports.

Introduction

I have loved baseball all my life. Some of my earliest memories are of rooting for the Los Angeles Dodgers against the New York Yankees in the 1977 World Series. I can still remember that great Dodgers infield of Steve Garvey at first base, Davey Lopes at second base, Bill Russell at shortstop, and "The Penguin" Ron Cey at third base.

Of this set of my then-favorite players, none made the Hall of Fame. None was the best ever at his position. In fact, I used to get into shouting matches about whether any of these folks was even the best player in 1977.

But even if these players weren't special to anyone else, they were special to me, because *I* rooted for them when I was a kid. Now, with an extra 30 years or so of perspective, I don't get upset when someone makes fun of Steve Garvey. Instead, I get upset when people don't recognize Johnny Bench as the greatest catcher in history.

The point is, I *care* about baseball. Other adults I know also take the game far more seriously than grown folks probably should. We watch major-league games, we talk about the games, we complain about the players, we stay up past 1 A.M. to see the Red Sox beat the Yankees (or vice versa). Why? Because we fell in love with the game when we were your age.

Since your parents were young, major-league baseball has evolved into new stadiums, with new league rules, new teams, and certainly different players. But the links to the past are always present. Maybe your mom's favorite player from when she was a girl is now managing somewhere. Perhaps you could go to a game at Wrigley Field in Chicago, where the Cubs have played since 1914—maybe your great-great-grandfather once attended a game there! Or you could listen to a Dodgers radio broadcast to hear broadcaster Vin Scully, who has been the voice of the Dodgers for 64 years.

The Everything® KIDS' Baseball Book, 8th Edition can be your guide to baseball past and baseball present. It's certainly fun to read straight through, but it can also be a useful reference. Are your grandparents always talking about the 1954 World Series? Read about what they saw in this book. Is your brother always staring at the box scores in the newspaper or online? Use this book to find out what those columns of numbers mean. Do you want to become a better player? This book gives you some ideas for developing your playing skills. Having trouble understanding your dad's fantasy baseball team? This book explains fantasy baseball, so you'll be able to give *him* pointers.

There's undoubtedly more to baseball than merely what is contained in this book. Appendix B, or your parents or a librarian, can suggest where to go to find more detail than what is included here. My simple hope is that by reading this book you can start to fall in love with baseball, just like I did years ago.

Chapter 1
Playing the Game

Baseball is a great game, one that is played and enjoyed by tens of millions of people. Many of those who appreciate the game grew up playing and watching baseball. Few get good enough to be a major leaguer, but everyone can learn how to play, and everyone can, with practice, become a better player. This chapter covers the fundamentals of baseball: the rules, the necessary skills, the positions of the players, and some ways to play baseball even if you don't have two teams of nine players available.

Rules of the Game

Baseball, at its heart, is a very simple game. A batter hits the ball, then tries to make it to first base (or farther!) without getting called out. Someone who gets all the way around the bases scores a run; whichever team scores the most runs during the game wins.

Teams take turns at bat. A team keeps batting until they make three outs; then they pitch to the other team until *they* make three outs. After each team has had nine turns, the game is over.

Here are the most common ways for the batter to make an out:

- **Strikeout.** A batter gets a strike if he swings and misses, or if he doesn't swing at a good pitch. Three strikes and the batter is out.
- **Flyout.** If a fielder catches a batted ball before it hits the ground, the batter is out.
- **Groundout.** If a fielder throws the ball to first base before the batter gets there, the batter is out.
- **Tagged out.** If a runner is not touching a base and is tagged with the ball, the runner is out.

WORDS to KNOW

inning: A turn at bat for each team is called an inning. A professional or college baseball game lasts for nine innings. High school and Little League games are usually shorter—five, six, or seven innings.

There's much, much more to the rules of baseball, but you learn by playing and watching the game. Even professional players are still learning about the game. That's part of what makes baseball such a wonderful sport!

Developing Your Baseball Skills

How can you develop your baseball skills? The answer is simple: play. Play a lot. Play with your friends, play in a league or two, play in the backyard with your family. The more you play, the more you'll learn about the game. You'll develop baseball instincts—you'll know what to do on the bases or in the field without even thinking about it. Your skills will get better and better. And whether or not you become a great player, you will likely develop a deep appreciation for the game of baseball that you can share with your friends and family. Many adults' most profound memories are of playing and watching baseball when they were kids your age.

For professional baseball you need two teams of nine players, each with uniforms and gloves, several brand-new baseballs, and some umpires . . . but all you *really* need to play a game is a few friends, an old tennis ball, and a stick for a bat.

Hitting

To become a good hitter, you have to hit—a lot. Of course you'll get to hit in games, but if you want to get more hitting practice, try these ideas:

- **Take a bucket of balls out to an empty field.** Have a friend pitch them all to you. Pick up all the balls and then you pitch them all to your friend.

> ## WORDS to KNOW
>
> **umpire:** Umpires referee baseball games. They decide all close calls. Is the pitch a ball or a strike? Is the runner safe or out? Is the ball fair or foul? The umpire's decision is final. A good umpire can make a game much more fun: since the ump makes all the close decisions, instead of arguing with the other team, you can spend your time playing the game.

FUN FACT

What Is a Slump?

A slump is when a hitter stops getting hits for a while. Slumps happen to all hitters, even the best. Usually a slump lasts for only a few games, but sometimes it will go on for weeks. Hitters will try everything from extra batting practice to good luck charms to get out of a slump. When you get in a slump, just relax and try not to get too frustrated—all slumps have to end sometime.

- **Get some Wiffle balls.** Wiffle balls are plastic balls with holes in them. Since they won't go far, they are less likely to hurt someone or something. Wiffle balls are good for playing on a small field or in the backyard.
- **Hit balls off of a tee.** You can practice hitting the ball in different directions: try hitting ten balls to left field, ten to center field, then ten to right field.
- **Go to a batting cage.** A machine will pitch a ball to you, and you can decide how fast you want the ball to come toward you.

Hitting Practice Is the Time to Experiment

Try out different kinds of bats—heavy bats, light bats, long bats, short bats, wooden bats, and metal bats. You don't necessarily have to buy yourself a brand-new bat to try it out. Ask to borrow a bat from a friend, or buy a cheap used bat at a secondhand store.

Then try different ways to stand. Mimic your favorite player's stance. Try out some of the advice a coach or a friend gave you. Find out what feels the most comfortable. As long as you can see the ball well, as long as you can keep your eye on the ball when you make contact, then your stance is fine. You may fine-tune it someday, but for now, go with what feels the best.

Most importantly, work on making contact with the ball. Don't worry about how hard you hit it—don't swing hard to hit home runs—just practice *hitting* the ball with every swing. After all this hitting practice, you'll find your hitting in games to be more consistent. Your body will know exactly what to do. You'll end up getting on base a lot. Eventually, without even trying, you'll start hitting the ball harder.

Defense

The team that isn't batting is called the defense. Their job is to field the ball and put the batters out. The nine players on defense play the different positions described in the following list. Each position requires slightly different skills, though all defensive players must be able to throw well.

- **Infielders.** Those who play first base, second base, third base, and shortstop are called infielders. Infielders play close to the batter and to the bases. They field ground balls and try to throw the batter out. When a ball is hit into the outfield, the infielders receive the ball from the outfielders and try to tag out runners.
- **Outfielders.** The right fielder, left fielder, and center fielder are the outfielders. They play far away from the batter and the bases. Their main job is to catch fly balls and to throw the ball back to the infielders.
- **Catcher.** The catcher crouches behind home plate to catch any pitches that the batter doesn't hit. If a runner tries to steal a base, the catcher tries to throw the runner out.
- **Pitcher.** The pitcher starts all the action on the field by throwing every pitch to the batter. Pitchers also have to field ground balls and help out the infielders.

The best way to improve your baseball skills is to play in lots of games. A fielder needs to develop a "baseball sense" in addition to physical skills. This means not just being able to field and throw the ball but knowing *where* to throw the ball and where to be on the field. When you're in the field, think to yourself before every pitch: If the ball comes to me, what do I do with it? If the ball doesn't come to me, where am I supposed to go? By answering these questions before every

WORDS to KNOW

choking up: Sometimes a coach will suggest that you choke up on the bat. This means to hold your hands higher above the end of the bat, as you can see in the picture. Choking up makes it easier to contact the ball, but more difficult to hit the ball hard.

ghost runner: You can play baseball with as few as two or three players per team. But what do you do if a three-player team loads the bases so that the next batter is standing on third base? You put a "ghost runner" on third. The other runners run the bases as normal, but everyone pretends that the ghost runner is running too. You should make rules ahead of time about how to put a ghost runner out!

pitch in every game you play, you will build up good baseball instincts that you may not even be aware of. You'll find yourself making great plays simply because you knew what to do before the batter even hit the ball.

Throwing

The most important defensive skill, regardless of position, is throwing. Everyone on the field needs to be able to throw accurately over short and long distances.

How do you get good at throwing? Practice. Find a friend, grab your gloves, and play catch. Don't throw as hard or as fast as you can; just stand at a comfortable distance and practice throwing the ball right to your friend. For example, see how many throws you can make to each other without dropping the ball. Once you can make 30 or 40 throws in a row, each of you take a big step back and try again.

If you want to practice throwing by yourself, find a heavy, solid wall, like the backboard at a tennis or handball court. Use chalk to lightly mark a square about chest high. Using a tennis ball, try to hit the wall inside the square. You can design a game—call a "strike" if the ball hits inside the square, call a "ball" if the ball hits on the line or outside the square. Try to earn a strikeout by throwing three strikes before you throw four balls. Once strikeouts become easy, take a step back and try again, or redraw a smaller square.

Fielding Ground Balls

When the batter hits a ground ball, the infielders try to pick up the ball, then throw to first base quickly to put the batter out. When you are developing your skill at fielding ground balls, don't worry about making the throw to first base. Start by making sure you can catch the ball every time.

Shuffle your feet to get your body in front of the ball; watch the ball all the way until it is inside your glove. Try to be in such a good position that anytime the ball takes a funny hop it hits you in the leg or in the chest and stops nearby. That way you'll still be able to pick the ball up quickly.

The way to get good at fielding grounders is (surprise!) to practice. Set up some bases with a couple of friends. Put one person at bat, one person at first base, and one person at shortstop. Have the batter hit ground balls toward the short-stop, who should field them and throw to first base. Keep this up until the shortstop successfully fields five or ten balls in a row, then rotate who gets to play shortstop. Two friends can also roll grounders to each other. You can even practice grounders by throwing a tennis ball against a wall and field-ing the rebound.

Catching Fly Balls

Outfielders especially have to practice fielding fly balls. The hardest part of catching flies is figuring out where the ball is headed. Once you know where the ball is going to land, run to that spot, turn toward the ball with your glove above your head, and catch the ball in front of you.

Try not to have to catch a ball while you're still running—this makes it harder to judge where the ball is, so it's more likely you'll drop it. Also, if you're running, it will be harder to make the throw back to the infield. Of course, sometimes a ball is hit so far away from you that the only way to catch it is to keep running as hard as you can the whole way. But if you can manage to stop before you catch the ball, do it.

Fly ball practice is best done with a real batter, not just with someone throwing the ball in the air. Try to get friends to hit fly balls to you, especially if you have some friends who are good batters. High school kids or adults can give the best fly

FUN FACT

Even Major Leaguers Practice

One time, the great San Diego hitter Tony Gwynn didn't get a hit in a game that lasted almost until midnight. According to baseball lore, on his way home, Gwynn stopped by his old high school, where he had a key to the batting cage. He prac-ticed hitting in the cage for about an hour before he went to bed.

WORDS to KNOW

pull hitter: A right-handed pull hitter tends to hit the ball to left field every time. (Of course, a left-handed pull hitter tends to hit to right field.) Pull hitters usually generate a lot of power, but they are easy to defend against. The best hitters can also hit to the opposite field—in other words, a right-handed hitter will be able to hit toward right field.

Little League Facts

Little League baseball began in 1939 in Williamsport, Pennsylvania, where the Little League World Series is still played today. Little League baseball! is popular with boys and girls of all ages, from all over the world. Teams usually have between 12 and 20 players on them, and everyone on a team should get a chance to play.

Cobb on Hitting

Ty Cobb was one of the best hitters ever. He recommended that hitters not hold the bat all the way at the bottom. He suggested holding the hands an inch from the knob and keeping the hands an inch apart from each other for better balance and bat control. Not everyone should hit this way, but Ty Cobb had a career .367 batting average and made the Hall of Fame, so his advice might work!

ball practice, because they might have better bat control to hit a lot of good fly balls.

Pitching

In the major leagues, pitchers are specialists—that is, their job is only to pitch, and they rarely work on any other skills or play any other positions. Major-league pitchers spend their practice time building arm and leg strength, practicing different types of pitches, and resting their arms.

When younger people play baseball, however, the pitcher is just a good player who can throw the ball accurately. Pitchers who aren't pitching usually play elsewhere in the field. It is far, far more important for a pitcher to be able to hit a target than for a pitcher to throw hard or to throw different pitches.

Professional pitchers throw 80, 90, or even 100 miles per hour; they throw curveballs, knuckleballs, sliders, and forkballs. But they are *professionals*. They are pitching to the best hitters in the world, so they must take every advantage they can find.

The best youth league and even high school pitchers don't necessarily throw hard or curvy stuff. They throw a fastball consistently to the catcher's glove every time whether the catcher asks for a pitch inside or outside, high or low.

What kind of pitch can you throw besides a fastball? Try a changeup. You normally grip a fastball with your thumb and your first two fingers. Instead, try holding the ball all the way back in your palm, but use the same motion as you do for a fastball. You should find that this pitch goes just a bit slower; that's a changeup. Changeups are hard to hit because they throw off the batter's timing—the batter will be starting to swing just before the ball gets to the plate. If you can throw just a fastball and changeup, and if you can throw them right

Why do hitters like night baseball?

Connect the dots to find the answer to the above riddle.

Because there are more

to choose from!

to the catcher's glove on every pitch, then you will be an outstanding young pitcher.

Baseball Fun Without a Full Team

If you're short on players or equipment but you really want to play a game of baseball, don't panic! There are a few alternatives that are similar to baseball that you can play when you only have a few friends available or you can't get your hands on a bat, ball, or glove.

Punchball

This game uses the same basic idea of baseball, but if you don't have gloves, bats, or a field handy, you can use a tennis ball, or even a heavy wad of taped-up paper. Throw the ball up above your head, then swing your extended arm like a bat and "punch" the ball. Position as many fielders as you have at bases and in the outfield. You don't need a pitcher or a catcher, and if you don't have enough people to fill the other positions, you can shrink the field and only play with three bases and two outfielders (it's hard to punch a ball into the outfield, anyway). Punchball is a good alternative to baseball or softball if you're looking for a baseball-like game to play with friends.

Two-Ball

This is a good baseball game for six to eight players. Divide the players into teams of two. Each pair takes a turn at bat while everyone else plays in the field. A pitcher pitches to a batter as in normal baseball. The batter hits the ball and runs to first, but the batter is out if any fielder can touch the ball before the batter reaches first base. Then the batter's partner bats.

Batting Cage Game

When you go to a batting cage, you usually get ten swings for a certain amount of money. You and a friend can have a friendly game of batting cage baseball. Here's how it works: Every time you make contact, you get one point, even if you hit a foul ball. Every time you hit the ball beyond the pitching machine, you get two points. Every time you miss the ball, you lose one point. This game helps you concentrate on making contact with the ball. As you make contact more and more, you'll feel comfortable taking bigger swings to get more two-pointers, but you may also miss and lose some points.

Curve Ball

The curve ball is one of the trickiest pitches to hit. See if you can score by running a line of color through each of the curvy baseball terms in the following list! Instead of reading in a straight line, each word has <u>one</u> bend in it. Words can go in any direction.

HINT: One word has been done for you.

ASTROTURF

~~BLEACHERS~~

DUGOUT

HOME RUN

HOT DOG

POP FLY

SCOREBOARD

SHORTSTOP

STADIUM

WORLD SERIES

```
F L Y L E B O A R D T O
U P O R R L E R N P O P
G R O M F E S E I R E S
A C U P D A T S C T M D
S S T G I C O S H I R L
T K R U U H H N D S N R
R B O E M O R E P U T O
I O U S R H O T R S G W
H O T T S T O P E S O O
O M D U U H O T M T U B
T D O L R K M M O A T L
R O G D B F E O H D M A
```

FUN FACT

Other "Little" Leagues

Even if you're not ready for official Little League ball, you might have other options. In tee-ball, there's no pitcher—the batter just hits the ball off of a tee. Other leagues allow coaches to pitch to the players or limit each inning to nine batters. Ask around to find out what kinds of leagues for young players are available in your community.

Catching with Style?

You might have seen a major leaguer make what looks like a cool catch on an easy play. For example, outfielder Dave Parker of the Pirates and Reds used to flip his glove down for a "snap catch." Although he was a Hall of Fame leadoff hitter and base-stealer, Rickey Henderson yanked his glove sideways when he caught fly balls. Any coach will tell you that making a fancy catch in a game is a *bad idea*—you could drop the ball!

The batting pair doesn't run the bases: base runners are ghost runners who advance whenever the batter gets a hit. After the batters make three outs, they go into the field, and the next pair comes in to bat. This is a fun but exhausting game. On offense, it will help you develop your ability to hit the ball where you want it to go; defenders will develop their range. Oh, and playing this game will help make sure you're in shape!

Off the Wall

This is a fun game you can play with two people, a ball, a glove, and a wall. You don't even need a glove if you're using a softer ball like a tennis ball.

Find a wall without windows where it's appropriate to throw a ball. You can use a vacant racquetball court, one wall of a gymnasium, or even the side of a barn. Next to the wall, mark off a territory to designate what is fair and what is foul. Use an area big enough that you can run from one end to the other in not too many steps. (Experiment to get the size right.)

To play, one player throws the ball high off the wall and the other person has to catch it. If the catcher catches the ball without it bouncing on the ground, he or she gets an "out." If the catcher drops it, the person throwing the ball has a runner on first base. If the ball bounces once before being caught, it's a single; twice, it's a double; three times, it's a triple; and four times, it's a home run. Always remember where your runners are, and keep track of how many runs you each score. Don't choose a space too big, or you'll never be able to cover the ground. Also, make a rule against throwing the ball so close to the wall that the only way to catch it is by crashing into the wall. Off the Wall is a good way to practice covering ground in the outfield and catching fly balls.

Chapter 2
The History of Baseball

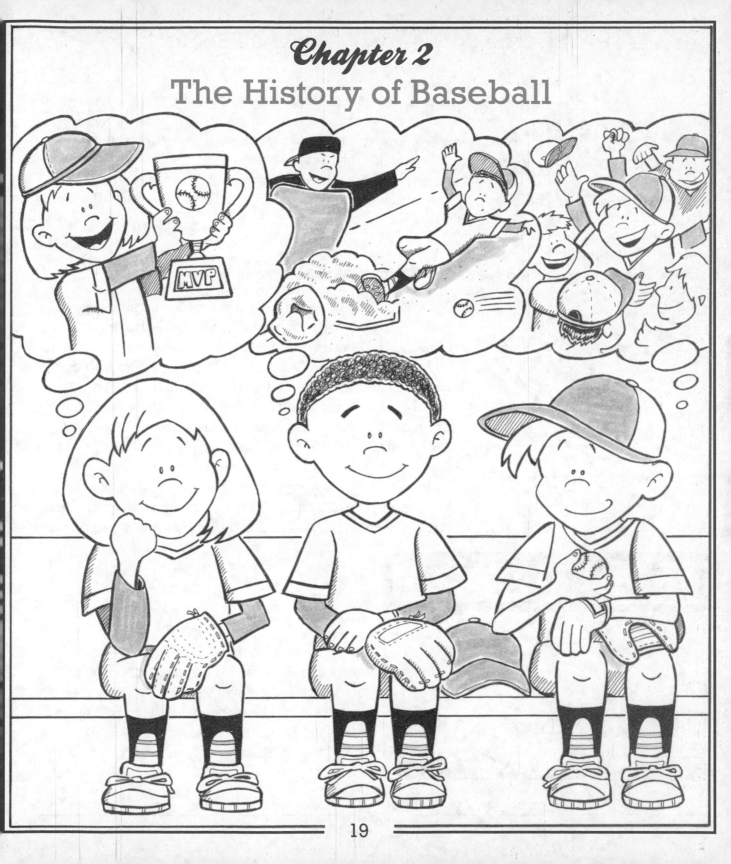

There are 30 major-league teams today, and many more minor-league teams with players hoping to make it to the big leagues. There are thousands of college teams, high school teams, and little league teams all playing baseball. But where did it all begin? How did the major leagues get started? This chapter will answer all your questions!

The Earliest Games

Baseball has been played for well over 150 years. The game became well known around the United States during and after the Civil War, in the 1860s. Back then, pitchers threw underhanded, no one had gloves, the ball was softer than what we know as a baseball today, and the bases were 42 paces (probably about 120 feet) from each other—but it was baseball. The idea was to hit the ball, get from base to base safely, and score runs before getting three outs in your team's turn at bat.

Amateur teams were formed, and they played until the first team scored 21 runs, which at that time only took a few innings. In 1857, the idea of playing a nine-inning game was introduced, the bases were placed 90 feet apart, and more rules were changed.

The First Professional Teams

As far back as the 1860s there were barnstorming teams, which were teams that went from city to city playing each other. The first of these teams to be made up entirely of paid players was the Cincinnati Red Stockings of 1869. That first professional team's record was 57-0. In

1871, the National Association of Professional Baseball Players was formed with nine teams. The Philadelphia Athletics were the first champions, winning 22 and losing only 7. By 1875 too much gambling caused people to lose interest in this league, but not in baseball. In 1876 the National League was formed. Many players from the original association became part of this new league, including Cap Anson, who was considered one of the game's first star players.

Through the 1880s and 1890s, several other leagues, including the American Association, the Players League, and a minor league called the Western League, began. All except the Western League failed.

Baseball Through the Decades

The modern era of baseball is said to have begun in 1900. Here is a look at what happened in baseball history in each of the decades of the 1900s and in the current century.

1900–1909

World Championships: Cubs (2), Boston Americans, New York Giants, White Sox, Pirates

Most Famous Players: Honus Wagner, Nap Lajoie, Ty Cobb, Cy Young, Christy Mathewson

In 1901, the Western League turned into the American League and started taking players from the National League. National League team owners were none too happy about this. The unfriendliness between the two leagues lasted for two years, until they finally united in 1903 and came up with the idea of a World Series between the two leagues.

box score: A box score is a grid containing a summary of each player's game statistics. Take a look at Chapter 8 to learn how to read a box score.

The Curse of the Bambino

Between 1903 and 1918, the Boston Red Sox won the World Series five times. Following the 1919 season, the Red Sox traded Babe Ruth ("the Bambino") to the New York Yankees. After the trade, the Red Sox didn't win another World Series for 86 years. They lost in the deciding game of the playoffs or World Series on six occasions. This misfortune is called the "Curse of the Bambino."

WORDS to KNOW

World Series: The winners of the National League and the American League have played the World Series each fall since 1903 (with two exceptions).

FUN FACT

The Box Score

In the 1850s, New York newspaper writer Henry Chadwick invented a clever way of summarizing the results of a baseball game. His invention, the box score, lists the game's players and what they did in their at bats or on the pitching mound. The box scores you read today are quite similar to the ones Henry Chadwick put together. You can learn how to read a box score in Chapter 8.

The first decade of the 1900s featured a great Chicago Cubs team that won 116 games and lost only 36 in 1906. They played in three World Series and won two of them. The Cubs featured an incredible infield combination that included Joe Tinker at shortstop, John Evers at second base, and Frank Chance at first base.

Nap Lajoie was the American League's first batting champion, with an incredible .422 batting average, topped only once ever since. Ty Cobb and Honus Wagner were great hitters and had tremendous speed, stealing plenty of bases. Pitching was very different then: there were only five or six pitchers on a team, and starters pitched more often and for more innings than they do today. Hitters hit plenty of singles, doubles, and even triples, but home runs were not common, and league leaders did not top 16 homers through 1910.

1910–1919

World Championships: Red Sox (4), Philadelphia A's (3), Boston Braves, White Sox, Reds

Most Famous Players: Ty Cobb, Tris Speaker, Gavvy Cravath, Walter Johnson, Joe Jackson

The United States was immersed in the First World War during the latter part of this decade. Yet baseball continued uninterrupted. The major leagues were challenged by a new league called the Federal League, which spent a couple of years taking players away from the American and National Leagues. Finally the major leagues were able to reach an agreement with this new league, which was dissolved. John McGraw, one of baseball's all-time great managers, led the NL's New York Giants to four World Series but no championships. In the American League, the Philadelphia Athletics, led by their great manager Connie Mack, and the Boston Red Sox were the toughest teams.

Walter Johnson won 20 or more games every year in this decade. He was truly a great pitcher. But pitching was certainly easier back in this "dead-ball era." Until about 1920, the ball was much squishier than the baseballs we play with today, and the same ball was usually used for the entire game. Gavvy Cravath of the Philadelphia Phillies led the National League in home runs six times—but he never hit more than 24 homers in a season.

1920–1929

World Championships: Yankees (3), New York Giants (2), Indians, Washington Senators, Pirates, Cardinals, Philadelphia A's

Most Famous Players: Rogers Hornsby, Babe Ruth, Lou Gehrig, Lefty Grove, Grover Alexander

After World War I, the country entered a period called the Roaring Twenties, filled with plenty of singing, dancing, and great baseball. The Yankees began their 40-year domination of the major leagues, during which they won 29 American League pennants and 20 world championships.

FUN FACT

Black Sox

In 1919 the Chicago White Sox earned the name "Black Sox." Eight players on the team were accused of being paid by gamblers to intentionally lose the World Series to the Reds. The first commissioner of baseball banned the eight players from the game forever. One of those players, Shoeless Joe Jackson, was one of baseball's all-time greatest hitters, but because he was kicked out of baseball, Jackson is not eligible for election to the Hall of Fame.

FUN FACT

Who Says Baseball Is a Slow Game?

World Series games in the first decade of the 1900s usually took about an hour and a half. That's amazing, considering that even regular season games today take close to three hours to play.

The dead-ball era was over in the 1920s. Though many sluggers emerged, it was Babe Ruth who captured the imagination of the fans. His record of 60 homers in 1927 stood for 34 years; his 714 career home runs were the most ever until 1974. "The Babe" was a big hero everywhere he went, and he was the first player to make as much as $50,000, which in those days was a very high salary—equivalent to at least half a million dollars in today's money. Whether it was because of all the home runs or not, baseball reached enormous popularity in the 1920s. In 1928, 61,000 people came to Yankee Stadium to watch the Yankees defeat the Cardinals in Game 1 of the World Series; nearly 40,000 attended Game 3 in the much smaller city of St. Louis. Baseball cemented its title as the national pastime.

Stealing Bases

These teams are some of the first baseball teams in this country! Some are still around, while some have moved to different cities and changed their names. See if you can finish the teams' names by adding the missing letters **B-A-S-E-S.**

```
_ _ L T I M O R _   O R I O L _ _
_ O _ T O N   R _ D   _ O X
N _ W   Y O R K   M _ T _
_ R O O K L Y N   D O D G _ R _
L O _   _ N G _ L E _   _ N G _ L _
_ T L _ N T _   _ R _ V E _
```

1930–1939

World Championships: Yankees (5), Cardinals (2), Philadelphia A's, New York Giants, Tigers

Most Famous Players: Lefty Grove, Lou Gehrig, Johnny Mize, Jimmie Foxx, Hack Wilson, Dizzy Dean, Hank Greenberg

The Great Depression made the 1930s difficult for many Americans. Many people were out of work and money was scarce. Baseball was an escape from the tough times. Jimmie Foxx of the Philadelphia A's came close to Ruth's home run record, hitting 58 homers in one season. The Cubs' Hack Wilson set a one-season record that still holds today, driving in 191 runs. Babe Ruth played his last game for the Yankees in 1934, and then played a few with the Braves in 1935 before retiring. Ruth's teammate Lou Gehrig continued to play alongside a new teammate who appeared in 1936, another baseball legend named Joe DiMaggio. Gehrig retired because of a serious illness in 1937 after playing in 2,130 consecutive games, a record that many thought would never be broken.

Another lasting change to the game took place in 1935 in Cincinnati when the first night game was played. The idea caught on fast, and pretty soon many night games appeared on the schedule—except at Wrigley Field in Chicago, where night games were not played until 1988.

FUN FACT

Murderer's Row

The greatest lineup in baseball history is thought to be the 1927 lineup of the New York Yankees, nicknamed "Murderer's Row." Here are the season stats of some of their best players. As you look at these, remember that in 1927 only five players hit more than 20 home runs and that 100 RBIs has always been considered to be a very good season. These guys were incredible!

Position	Name	AVG	HR	RBI
1B	Lou Gehrig	.373	47	175
2B/3B/SS	Tony Lazzeri	.309	18	102
LF	Bob Meusel	.337	8	103
CF	Earle Combs	.356	6	64
RF	Babe Ruth	.356	60	164

Uniform Numbers

The Yankees were the first team to wear numbers on their backs in the 1920s. They started out by assigning numbers based on the batting order: Babe Ruth always hit third, so he was number 3, Lou Gehrig always hit fourth, so he was number 4, and so on. Today the number on a player's uniform is only used to identify the player and has nothing to do with where the player bats.

FuN FACT

Retired Numbers

A team will sometimes retire the number of a famous player. This means that no one else on that team ever wears the retired number again—for example, the Cincinnati Reds retired Johnny Bench's number 5, so a Reds uniform with 5 on it will forever be associated with Bench. The Yankees have retired 16 different uniform numbers, the most of any team.

Travel by Train

Today, most teams get from one city to the other in a few hours by private jet. But through much of baseball's history, teams took trains on their road trips. That's the main reason why there were no major-league teams out west or in the South—a trip just from New York to Chicago meant sitting (and sleeping) on the train for an entire day.

1940–1949

World Championships: Yankees (4), Cardinals (3), Reds, Tigers, Indians

Most Famous Players: Warren Spahn, Johnny Sain, Ted Williams, Joe DiMaggio, Bob Feller

World War II was the country's main focus in the first half of the 1940s, and many ballplayers left their teams to serve in the United States military. Young players and veterans who were too old for the military made up most of the teams. Since many of the men were in the army, women's baseball teams emerged, attracting a lot of attention as they played in their own league. The movie A *League of Their Own* is based on this 1940s women's baseball league.

Even though most young American people were off to war, baseball remained an important part of their lives. Soldiers were proud of their hometown teams, and they kept track of events in the major leagues as best they could. The infantrymen even used baseball questions to distinguish friend from foe. They say that General Omar Bradley once nearly failed to convince a lookout that he was an American soldier because he didn't know that the Brooklyn Dodgers played in the National League.

Most soldiers returned from the war in 1945 and 1946, and the best athletes went into (or back into) major-league baseball. Ted Williams, Joe DiMaggio, and Bob Feller were among the most well-known baseball and military heroes of the day. Williams in particular had already established himself as a great hitter, batting .406 in 1941. No one has batted over .400 since then. Though he took three years off from baseball, Williams returned to the game in 1946 and batted over .300 every year until 1959.

Winning World War II required a full effort from all segments of American society. Afterward, many thought it ridiculous that black men were allowed to risk their lives in battle but were not allowed (among other things) to play major-league baseball. Many great players, including Jackie Robinson, Cool Papa Bell, Josh Gibson, and Satchel Paige played in the Negro Leagues. There were many great players in these leagues, a number of whom would have been big stars in the major leagues if only the team owners would have let them play. In 1947, well before the civil rights movement of the 1960s, Brooklyn Dodgers general manager Branch Rickey promoted Jackie Robinson to the majors, thus breaking the "color barrier" and paving the way for the thorough integration of professional baseball over the next decades.

The Negro Leagues

The National League was formed in 1876, and in the early years of baseball people of any race could play. In fact, Moses Fleetwood Walker joined the Toledo ball club in 1884 as the first black professional ballplayer, and others followed. But these players were treated badly by fans, opposing players, and their own teammates. Besides calling them names, white pitchers would often throw knockdown pitches at them. Little by little, there were fewer and fewer black players in baseball. There was no written rule, but owners no longer signed black players. Such informal—yet real—discrimination was typical in most parts of American society for a large part of the 20th century.

Since it was becoming impossible to get into the major leagues, black players (referred to in those days as Negroes) began forming their own teams in the 1890s. By the early 1900s these teams were playing independently all over the eastern United States in cities like New York and Philadelphia. These teams often played exhibition games against major-league teams, and they did well. It was obvious that many of

Youngest Player Ever

In 1944, when most of the country's young men were involved in the war effort, 15-year-old Joe Nuxhall pitched in a game for the Cincinnati Reds to become the youngest major leaguer ever. Nuxhall was quickly sent back down to the minor leagues, but he rejoined the Reds in 1952 and played in the majors for 15 years.

Spahn and Sain

Warren Spahn and Johnny Sain led the pitching staff of the 1948 Boston Braves. Manager Billy Southworth wished he could let them pitch every day. So Gerald V. Hern of the *Boston Post* wrote a poem about them. The poem "Spahn and Sain and Pray for Rain" lives on in baseball's collective memory as a popular slogan for the '48 Braves.

Hard Ball

Baseball is a game full of action! Fill in as many wild words as you can, using the across and down clues. We left you some T-O-U-G-H letters and words as hints!

ACROSS

3. Fun baseball game played against an upright surface.

6. Team name: Pittsburgh

7. Nickname for a powerful hitter.

11. Smooth, round stick used to hit a baseball.

13. The 37-foot-high-wall in Boston's Fenway Park.

16. A "_____ hitter" is a hitter who hits for someone else.

17. To run from one base to another before the next player at bat has hit the ball.

19. Team name: San Francisco _____.

21. If the hitter bunts with a man on third base, it's called a "_____ play."

DOWN

1. Joe DiMaggio's nickname: "_____ in' Joe."

2. When a hitter stops getting hits for a while.

4. Hank Aaron's nickname: "The _____."

5. "The _____" is when fans stand and then sit while moving their arms up and down in a motion that goes all around the stadium.

6. A "_____" fly goes high up in the air and is easily caught.

7. Sharp bumps on the bottom of baseball players' shoes.

8. "The Seventh Inning _____" gives fans a chance to get up and move around.

9. Team name: Los Angeles _____.

10. The score made by a player who touches first, second, third, and home base.

11. Jose Canseco and Mark McGwire were known as the "_____ Brothers."

12. A ball hit out of fair territory.

14. A _____ play is when a player is trapped between two bases. He has to scramble to get to one base or the other before being tagged out.

15. A "_____ ball" is the speediest pitch.

18. A player will sometimes have to _____ headfirst into a base to avoid being tagged out.

20. A "grand_____" is a home run hit when bases are loaded.

the players on these teams had the talent to play in the major leagues, but the practice of discrimination was too strong.

Teams in the Negro Leagues faced major problems, such as finding places to play. The teams often had to rent stadiums from white owners, who didn't always treat them fairly. Many owners did not allow them to use the "white" locker rooms. Nonetheless, the teams persisted, with players playing for the love of the game more than anything else, since most weren't making much money.

The Great Depression in the 1930s marked the end of the early Negro Leagues. Most of the teams, which had a hard time making money, had to call it quits. But touring teams such as the Pittsburgh Crawfords and Washington, D.C.'s Homestead Grays managed to play. Many major leaguers had great respect for the black ballplayers and still played exhibition games against these touring teams. By the late 1930s, as the country's economy improved, the Negro Leagues were back with new teams.

In the 1940s, Branch Rickey became determined to sign the first black major leaguer, despite the feelings of the other team owners. Rickey owned the Brooklyn Brown Bombers, a team in the Negro Leagues, and he was also the president and general manager of the Brooklyn Dodgers. In 1946, Rickey watched the Kansas City Monarchs come to town with a young player named Jackie Robinson. Rickey signed Robinson to a minor league contract in 1945, and called him up as a member of the Dodgers in 1947.

As more black players made the major leagues, there was less of a need for the Negro Leagues. While many of the greatest Negro League stars never made it to the major leagues, the leagues gave these ballplayers a place to show their great talents. It would eventually serve as a showcase for players to get to the major leagues. You can't help but

Rookie of the Year

Since Jackie Robinson in 1947, the best first-year player in each league has been honored with the Rookie of the Year award.

FuN FACT

Why Brooklyn?

New York City consists of five large sections called boroughs. Unlike the Yankees and Giants, the Dodgers claimed to represent only one of these five boroughs, Brooklyn. But Brooklyn by itself was larger than any other American city except for Chicago!

wonder how some of the great major leaguers might have
fared in daily competition against all of the country's best
athletes, not just those who happened to be white.

Famous Negro Leaguer: Satchel Paige, 1926–1953

W-L	ERA	K
28-31	3.29	288

Major-league totals only

Satchel Paige was a genuine baseball superstar. He had
a long career, during which an estimated 10 million people
watched him pitch—in person, since he played most of his
games before they were shown on television! Paige played for
a variety of Negro Leagues teams from 1926 to 1947, moving from team to team depending on who could pay him the
most money. Americans, black or white, were willing to pay to
see Paige pitch. His reputation as one of the greatest pitchers
in baseball was well established before World War II, during
which he raised money for the war effort through his pitching exhibitions. He played with Negro Leagues all-stars in
competitive exhibition games against major leaguers. Finally,
after Jackie Robinson broke in with the Dodgers, Paige was
signed to a major-league contract with the Cleveland Indians
in 1948 at age 42. He played two seasons with the Indians,
then moved with owner Bill Veeck to the St. Louis Browns,
where he made the all-star team. His career totals look poor
compared to the other pitchers in this list, but bear in mind
that Paige put up these numbers over only five seasons, and
he was 47 years old during that last season. One can only
imagine the kind of career stats Paige could have earned had
he played all of those 27 years in the major leagues.

Rube Foster

Rube Foster was one of the great
pitchers of the early 1900s. He pitched
for the 1906 Philadelphia Giants and
went on to found the Negro National
Leagues which debuted in 1920 with
eight teams. In 1923, Foster helped
start a second league with six new
teams.

Paige on Age

Satchel Paige, who pitched for nearly
30 years and even appeared in a major-
league game at the age of 59, once
said, "Age is a case of mind over matter. If you don't mind, it don't matter."

1950–1959

World Championships: Yankees (6), New York Giants, Milwaukee Braves, Brooklyn Dodgers, Los Angeles Dodgers

Most Famous Players: Willie Mays, Mickey Mantle, Duke Snider, Ted Williams, Whitey Ford, Stan Musial

The City of New York dominated baseball. Their three teams—the Yankees, the Giants, and the Dodgers—were the best in the game, and they competed for the city's attention. One of the most memorable moments from those New York rivalries occurred at the end of the 1951 season. The New York Giants and the Brooklyn Dodgers were tied for first place in the NL, so they played a best-of-three playoff to see which team would go to the World Series. The Dodgers led the third game 4-1 going into the bottom of the ninth inning.

The Giants got one run to make the score 4-2, then Bobby Thomson came to bat against pitcher Ralph Branca with two men on base. Thomson hit a home run to left field, winning the game 5-4 and sending the Giants to the World Series. On the radio, Giants announcer Russ Hodges conveyed the fans' excitement with his famous call, shouting over and over, "The Giants win the pennant! The Giants win the pennant!" Thomson's home run became known as the "shot heard round the world."

In the 1950s, refrigerators, washing machines, and other new technologies began to change the way Americans lived. Two new technologies caused lasting changes in major-league baseball. The first was the beginning of televised baseball. Though virtually every game can be seen on TV today, in the early 1950s most people didn't even own television sets. But by the end of the decade, millions of

people could watch a baseball game even when they couldn't physically go to the game.

It might have been the jet airplane that ended the great New York baseball rivalries. By the end of the 1950s, travel by jet was common, meaning that people could get from the East Coast to the West Coast in less than a day. And, after World War II, the population of California grew very rapidly. To take advantage of the many potential new fans, both the Dodgers and the Giants moved to the West Coast in 1958— the Dodgers to Los Angeles, the Giants to San Francisco.

1960–1969

World Championships: Yankees (2), Dodgers (2), Cardinals (2), Pirates, Orioles, Tigers, Mets

Most Famous Players: Bob Gibson, Sandy Koufax, Don Drysdale, Hank Aaron, Frank Robinson, Willie McCovey, Carl Yastrzemski

New York maintained its reign as the focus of the baseball world, as the Yankees played in the World Series in 1960–1964. Yankee outfielder Roger Maris dueled with teammate Mickey Mantle for the 1961 home run crown— Maris hit number 61 on the last day of the season, breaking Babe Ruth's hallowed record.

The 1960s were a time of expansion. The number of teams in each league hadn't changed for many decades. But in 1961, the American League added two new teams: the Los Angeles Angels and the Washington Senators. A year later, the National League added two new teams, the New York Mets and the Houston Colt .45s, who became the Astros. New teams are usually not very good, but in 1962 the Mets won only 40 games while losing 120. This was the worst record ever, and the Mets were greeted with many appropriate jokes.

WORDS to KNOW

pennant: The team that represents the National League or the American League in the World Series is said to have won the pennant.

The Asterisk

When Babe Ruth hit his 60 homers in 1927, teams played 154 games in a season. But in 1961, the American League changed to a 162-game schedule— Roger Maris had eight extra games to beat the Babe's record! Commissioner Ford Frick decreed that Maris's record of 61 homers should be listed with an asterisk indicating the extra games that Maris played.

League Championship Series

Until 1969, whichever team won the most regular-season games in each league went to the World Series. But starting in 1969, the leagues were split into divisions. The League Championship Series, or LCS, was played between the division winners. So today, the ALCS and the NLCS decide which team in each league goes to the World Series.

Baseball expanded by four more teams in 1969: the Montreal Expos and San Diego Padres in the National League, the Seattle Pilots (who became the Milwaukee Brewers after just one year) and Kansas City Royals in the American League. The 12-team leagues were split into two 6-team divisions, East and West.

Now you're probably wondering what happened to those terrible Mets. Well, after being pretty dreadful for seven years, they shocked the world in 1969. The same year that people landed on the moon for the first time ever, the Mets beat the Baltimore Orioles in five games to win the World Series.

1970–1979

World Championships: A's (3), Pirates (2), Reds (2), Yankees (2), Orioles

Most famous players: Reggie Jackson, Joe Morgan, Willie Stargell, Tom Seaver, Catfish Hunter, Pete Rose, Johnny Bench

Just 35 years ago, the major leagues were very different than they are today. For one thing, players could not be "free agents." Once a player was assigned to a team, he could not change teams unless he was traded or released. In 1972 the Major League Baseball players went on strike; they won the right to free agency a few years later.

Teams didn't usually score as many runs as they do today, and owners wanted to increase scoring. For example, in the American League in 1970, teams averaged 4.2 runs per game; in 2008, they averaged 4.6 runs per game. They had already lowered the height of the pitching mound in 1968, from 15 inches to its current height of 10 inches. So, in 1973 the American League introduced the "designated hitter."

Many teams moved into bigger stadiums in the 1970s, most of which used the same AstroTurf that the Astros put inside their dome. Turf caused the baseball to take high bounces, forcing fielders to adjust their positioning. Speed became a more important part of the game. In 1977, Lou Brock became the first player ever to steal 900 bases, breaking Ty Cobb's previous record of 892. (Rickey Henderson has since passed them both.) Most of these old stadiums were shaped like enormous concrete circles and were also used for football games, concerts, rodeos, and other big events. Tickets were much cheaper than they are now. In those days, a $5 ticket might be considered outrageously expensive; if a $5 ticket is available today, it's as a special discount.

On April 8, 1974, Hammerin' Hank Aaron of the Atlanta Braves hit his 715th career home run, one more than Babe Ruth hit. Aaron went on to finish his career where he began it, in Milwaukee, with 755 homers.

1980–1989

World Championships: Dodgers (2), Phillies, Cardinals, Orioles, Tigers, Royals, Mets, Twins, A's

Most Famous Players: Ozzie Smith, Nolan Ryan, Dennis Eckersley, Mike Schmidt, George Brett, Wade Boggs, Tony Gwynn, Rickey Henderson

Free agency caused player salaries to increase rapidly. In response, owners tried to limit players' abilities to change teams, and baseball players went on strike in the middle of the 1981 season. More than 700 games were canceled, and when baseball finally returned, the season was split into two halves. The winners of the first half played the winners of the second half in a special playoff series. Fans were not happy and did not watch much baseball on television or at the park in the second part of the 1981 season.

Baseball recovered as the decade went on. Half of the 26 teams played in at least one World Series in the 1980s, and

Best Record, No Reward

The team with the best record in the 1981 season was the Cincinnati Reds. However, because of the strike and the split season, they didn't make it to the World Series; they didn't even make it to the playoffs. They finished second to the Dodgers in the first half and second to the Astros in the second half.

WORDS to KNOW

designated hitter: A designated hitter (DH) is a player who bats for the pitcher. The American League uses the DH, but the National League does not—NL pitchers must bat for themselves. Since pitchers aren't usually good at hitting, this means more runs are usually scored in AL games.

Family Affair

At one time, Cal Ripken Jr. and his brother Billy both played for the Baltimore Orioles, with their dad as coach. In 1987 and 1988, their dad was also the manager.

nine different teams won championships. Speed continued to be a critical element of strategy, as pitchers had a hard time preventing the stolen base. In 1981, Rickey Henderson, king of the stolen base, stole a record 130 bases in one season.

The art of base stealing peaked in the 1980s, but the art of relief pitching was only beginning. Until the 1970s, it was normal for the starting pitcher to pitch the whole game. Relief pitchers, whose specific role was to pitch only the late innings, became much more specialized in the 1980s. Most teams began to use a "closer," a relief pitcher with the job of finishing just the last inning or two. Toward the end of the decade, teams began to use "setup" relievers, who relieved the starter in the seventh or eighth inning but gave way to the closer in the ninth.

1990–1999

World Championships: Yankees (3), Blue Jays (2), Reds, Twins, Braves, Marlins

Most Famous Players: Greg Maddux, Tom Glavine, John Smoltz, Randy Johnson, Cal Ripken Jr., Barry Bonds, Mark McGwire

The major leagues expanded even more in the 1990s with the addition of the Florida Marlins, Colorado Rockies, Arizona Diamondbacks, and Tampa Bay Devil Rays. This brought the number of major-league teams to today's total of 30. The play-off structure was changed once again in 1994, to the present format. Each league was split into three divisions—East, Central, and West.

In 1995, Cal Ripken Jr. of the Orioles played in his 2,131st consecutive game, breaking the record Lou Gehrig set in 1939. The September 6 game drew a sellout crowd, which included the president of the United States, and millions

of fans around the world watched on TV. Ripken ended his streak in 1998, after playing 2,632 consecutive games.

In one of the saddest episodes in baseball history, a strike ended the 1994 baseball season in August. It was the first time since 1904 that there was no postseason, no World Series, and no championship team. Millionaire players and millionaire team owners got very little sympathy from the fans, who were unhappy that they couldn't watch and enjoy their favorite game. When baseball returned in 1995, attendance was way down. For the next couple of seasons many fans were turned off to baseball.

In 1997, baseball owners decided that they'd try to draw fans back by starting interleague play, which meant regular season games between National and American League teams. Longtime baseball fans weren't happy about it, but on June 12, 1997, the Texas Rangers and the San Francisco Giants played in the first interleague game. What at first appeared to be a novelty caught on as cross-town rivals like the Cubs and White Sox in Chicago, the A's and Giants in neighboring Oakland and San Francisco, and the Mets and Yankees in New York all faced each other during the season.

Starting in the mid-1990s, players hit more home runs than ever before. In 1983, Mike Schmidt hit 40 home runs to lead the league. But in 1996, 40 home runs was only good for 12th best in the majors. In 1998, two players hit more home runs in the season than ever before. Sammy Sosa hit 66 and Mark McGwire hit 70, both breaking the single-season record of 61 Roger Maris had held since 1961.

There are several possible reasons for this offensive explosion. For one thing, players took weight training more seriously than ever before. In the 1980s, many teams did not even have their own weight rooms—players

The Nasty Boys

The Reds of the 1990s used a combination of outstanding relief pitchers. Randy Myers, Rob Dibble, and Norm Charlton regularly held late-inning Reds leads. Two of these three "Nasty Boys," Dibble and Myers, were named most valuable player (MVP) of the 1990 NLCS.

on the road had to find a local gym if they wanted to work out. But by the 1990s, teams built gyms, hired athletic trainers, and reaped the benefits of regular workouts. A second possible reason was the league's expansion. The addition of four new teams meant that more than 40 pitchers who previously weren't good enough to play in the majors were now pitching to the world's best power hitters.

But in the early 2000s, it came to light that many players were using illegal drugs called anabolic steroids to build their muscles. Sluggers Ken Caminiti and Jose Canseco came forward to tell of their own steroid use and to warn that many others were also using the same drugs. Only a few players directly admitted to using steroids. However, Barry Bonds was investigated by the FBI and Mark McGwire and Sammy Sosa were called to testify before Congress about their own steroid use. It's still not clear exactly which players were using steroids. But in 2005, the major leagues instituted steroid testing for all players. Since then, players have been hitting fewer home runs than they did a decade ago.

2000–2009

World Championships: Red Sox (2), Yankees (2), Diamondbacks, Angels, Marlins, Cardinals, Phillies, White Sox

Most Famous Players: Pedro Martinez, Roger Clemens, Johan Santana, Manny Ramirez, Albert Pujols, Randy Johnson, Ichiro Suzuki, Chipper Jones

The terrorist attacks of 2001 put a halt to baseball, but only for a week. The sport, and especially the Yankees' berth in the 2001 World Series, served as a rallying point for American culture. Since 2001, many teams have replaced

WORDS to KNOW

wild card: The winner of each division earns a spot in the playoffs. Also, a fourth and fifth team in each league play each other a one-game "wild card" showdown, with the winners advancing to the respective quarterfinal series. The wild card survivors have the same chance to win the World Series as any other playoff team; in fact, a wild card team won the championship five times in the first eight years since becoming eligible for the postseason.

the traditional singing of "Take Me Out to the Ball Game" during the seventh-inning stretch with "God Bless America."

The Chicago Cubs haven't won a World Series since 1908; the Boston Red Sox hadn't won since 1918. Both teams have been considered cursed for as long as most people can remember. In 2003, both teams were very good, and both seemed to have a good chance to make the World Series. But both faltered in the playoffs. The Cubs are still waiting for their championship, but the Red Sox earned their revenge in 2004. In the ALCS, they fell behind to the Yankees three games to none, but they came all the way back to win four games to three. Then they swept the St. Louis Cardinals to win their first World Series in 86 years.

Throughout the 2000s, the New York teams spent money like crazy trying to win. But they couldn't quite seem to beat teams with smaller payrolls. The decade began with a subway series between the Yankees and Mets in 2000. The Yankees made the playoffs every year from 2000–2007 but couldn't win another championship until 2009; the Mets only returned to the playoffs once, and they blew big division leads in both 2007 and 2008. In the 2000s, teams learned that spending money is less important than spending money wisely.

The biggest change to the game in the 2000s was in its national exposure. When your parents were growing up, they could see the home team and one or two other games of the week on television. That was it. In the 1990s, cable television allowed people to watch a bit more baseball. But then it became possible to see every game every night on the Internet, or on satellite television. Every radio broadcast could be heard on the Internet, or on satellite radio. The Internet allows instant access to box scores and stories about every game. Fantasy baseball is growing in popularity, once again due to the Internet.

FUN FACT

The Minor Leagues

Each major-league team supports several minor-league teams, which played through the strike of 1994. Almost every player spends a few years in the minors before coming to the major leagues. Some players are sent back down to the minor leagues if they are not playing well, and sometimes good major-league players will go to the minors after an injury to get used to playing again. Minor-league teams are in many smaller cities across the country.

2010–

World Championships: Giants (2), Cardinals, Red Sox

Most Famous Players: Miguel Cabrera, Buster Posey, Justin Verlander, Joey Votto, Josh Hamilton, Mike Trout, Robinson Cano

The decade began with the San Francisco Giants' first World Championship since they moved to California, and they added a second World Series title two years later. Meanwhile, their archrivals, the Los Angeles Dodgers, filed for bankruptcy under owner Frank McCourt before he sold the team to a group that included former basketball star Magic Johnson. The new owners spent a lot of money signing talented players and, despite a rash of injuries in the first half of 2013, the team made an inspired run in the second half with the return to health of Hanley Ramirez, and the addition of Cuban phenom Yasiel Puig.

In the American League, the Rangers made the first two World Series appearances in franchise history in consecutive years, but fell short of a championship by a single strike to the Cardinals in 2011.

Two new ballparks opened in the early part of the decade, but neither had a positive impact on their teams. The Twins did earn a third division title in five years during their first season at open-air Target Field in Minnesota, but sank to the bottom of the AL Central in following years. Despite the addition of highly paid free agents in 2012, the Marlins suffered through a disastrous initial season at futuristic Marlins Park and sold off some of their best players before 2013.

Baseball, in general, became more available to the public. A cell phone app allows fans to listen to or watch any

FUN FACT

Following a Game on the Internet

Several sites, including MLB.com, allow you to see the status of a game as it happens, who's at bat, who's pitching, lineups, a live box score, and much more.

Say What?

Yogi Berra was known as being quite a talker behind the plate. He hoped his chatter would distract the batter! The story goes that in the 1958 World Series, with the legendary Hank Aaron hitting, Yogi kept telling Aaron to "hit with the label up on the bat." Finally, Aaron couldn't stand it any more. He turned to Yogi and said "_____!"

To find out what Hank Aaron said to Yogi Berra, figure out where to put each of the cut-apart pieces of the grid.

C'mon Hank, hit it with the label up. Up, up, up, with the label up. C'mon Hank, hit it with the label up...

game. Podcasts offer highlights of games from the previous day. Sites like *www.baseball-reference.com* provide fans with the ability to study pitch-by-pitch recaps from any game in any season. Yet, with all its technological advancements, baseball remains the same game your parents played and watched when they were your age. Savor the games you watch now. Someday, your own grandchildren might be asking you about your favorite baseball memories.

Chapter 3
The National League

Baseball today is played by all sorts of teams, organized into youth leagues, high school districts, college conferences, semipro leagues, and minor leagues. The best-known teams play in the major leagues: the National League and the American League. Some of these teams, like the Dodgers and Yankees, have been around since well before even your great-grandparents were born. Others are as few as 10 years old. In this chapter, you can read about every National League team—including, perhaps, your favorite team.

The Start of the National League

In the 1870s, the National Association, one of the first professional baseball leagues, was having trouble. The team owners weren't following the league rules. The Boston Red Stockings seemed to win all the time. There was some shady business with gamblers who might have been fixing games. William Hulbert, owner of the Chicago White Stockings, convinced seven other owners to join with him in a new league: the National League. Only two of the teams are still playing today.

The Original 1876 National League

1876 Team Name	Modern Team Name
Chicago White Stockings	Chicago Cubs
Philadelphia Athletics	The Philadelphia Athletics only played in the NL in 1876
Boston Red Stockings	Atlanta Braves
Hartford Dark Blues	The Hartford Dark Blues only played in the NL in 1876 and 1877

1876 Team Name	Modern Team Name
Mutual of New York	Mutual of New York only played in the NL in 1876
St. Louis Brown Stockings	The St. Louis Brown Stockings only played in the NL in 1876 and 1877
Cincinnati Red Stockings	These Cincinnati Red Stockings only played in the NL from 1876–1880
Louisville Grays	The Louisville Grays only played in the NL in 1876 and 1877

Teams frequently joined and left the National League, especially in its early years. After the Houston Astros moved to the American League in 2013, the National League has 15 teams.

San Francisco Giants

Founded in 1883
Other names: New York Gothams, New York Giants
7 World Championships (1905, 1921, 1922, 1933, 1954, 2010, 2012)
19 NL pennants

Even though the Giants have played in San Francisco for all of your lifetime, and probably for all of your parents' lives, they were associated with the city of New York in their early days. During that time, their foremost rivals were the cross-town Brooklyn Dodgers. Both teams moved to California following the 1957 season.

The Windiest Ballpark

Candlestick Park, which was the home of the Giants for 40 years before the construction of AT&T Park in 2000, was built in an unsheltered area along San Francisco Bay. Candlestick was known for being very windy and cold, even in the summer. If you watch any old Giants games there, you'll see hot dog wrappers (and fly balls) blowing all over the place and fans huddling under blankets. In the midst of the 1961 All-Star Game at Candlestick, slight relief pitcher Stu Miller was stopped midpitch by a gust of wind.

"He's Always There"

Former Dodger player and manager Gil Hodges talked about how good a defensive player Willie Mays really was. "I can't very well tell my hitters, don't hit it to him. Wherever they hit it, he's always there."

Although the Dodgers won a World Championship in their second year on the West Coast, the Giants had to wait, and wait some more. Despite the presence of several Hall of Fame players, despite eight previous trips to the playoffs and three previous World Series appearances while representing San Francisco, it took the Giants more than a half-century to claim their first championship in California. But now, it's become a habit.

Two years after their breakthrough in 2010, the Giants won again, thanks to exceptional pitching performances. Tim Lincecum, who won two games as a starter in the 2010 Series, pitched 4⅔ innings of scoreless relief in the 2012 Series, a four-game sweep over the Tigers. Pablo Sandoval, benched in 2010, tied a Series record with three home runs in Game 1 of 2012, including two off the great Justin Verlander. A major influence in both years was catcher Buster Posey, the NL Rookie of the Year in 2010 and the NL Most Valuable Player two years later.

Famous Giant: Willie Mays, 1951–1973

HR	RBI	AVG
660	1,903	.302

Amazing Mays

A Giants broadcaster, in awe of one of Mays's hits, said "The only player who could have caught that ball, hit it."

He was known as the "Say Hey Kid" and was one of the greatest and most likable players to ever play the game. After his rookie season in 1951, Mays spent two years in the army before returning to the (then New York) Giants, with whom he racked up 41 homers and won the World Championship over the Cleveland Indians. Willie could do it all. He hit for power, leading the league in homers four times, and he also had great speed, leading the league in stolen bases four times. He was known for incredible defense; with his

basket catch, he used the glove as a "basket" to catch fly balls at his waist. Perhaps the most famous catch Mays ever made came in the first game of the 1954 World Series as he grabbed a ball going over his head in the deepest part of center field to help the Giants hold on and win. After many years with the Giants in San Francisco, Mays spent his last couple of years back in New York with the Mets before retiring as the third-greatest home run hitter ever. A baseball legend, Mays made the Hall of Fame in 1979.

Philadelphia Phillies

Founded in 1883
Other names: Philadelphia Quakers, Philadelphia Blue Jays
2 World Championships (1980, 2008)
7 NL pennants

Who Was the Most Famous Giant?

In this chapter, you'll read short notes about famous players on some teams. But since baseball has been around for such a long time, there are way more players than there is room to write about them. If you want to learn more about famous players on your favorite team, check out the *Baseball Encyclopedia*.

The Phillies' last World Championship, in 2008, occurred in the same season they achieved something less memorable: they lost a game for the 10,000th time in club history, a record for an American sports franchise. The franchise has had more than its share of bad years—twice in its history, the Phillies have gone more than a decade without a winning season.

But the 21st century has been the best of times for the team. Not only did the Phillies upgrade their home park from multipurpose Veterans Stadium, with its rock-hard artificial turf, to beautiful baseball-only Citizens Bank Park, but they also reeled off five consecutive division titles, including back-to-back trips to the World Series in 2008 and 2009. Behind the hitting of Ryan Howard and Chase Utley, and the relief pitching of Brad Lidge, who was a perfect 41-for-41 in save situations during the regular season and 7-for-7 in the postseason, the Phillies won their second championship in 2008.

Boo!

Philadelphia is known as a tough town in which to be a sports star. The fans take pride in yelling "Boo!" all the time. In fact, even though Phillies fans worship Mike Schmidt as one of their town's best professional athletes ever, the Veterans Stadium crowd once booed him. But that shouldn't make him feel too bad—Philadelphia fans famously booed Santa Claus at a football game!

Famous Phillie: Mike Schmidt, 1972–1989

HR	RBI	AVG
548	1,595	.267

Many baseball fans consider Mike Schmidt to be the best all-around third baseman ever to play the game. He was a truly awesome power hitter, leading the league eight times in home runs. In just 17 years he placed himself among the top ten all-time leaders in homers, won three MVPs, and helped lead the Phillies to their first ever World Championship. On the other side of the field, he was a tremendous defensive player. He won the Gold Glove as the best-fielding third baseman in the National League nine times. He went about his business very seriously, and fans and players alike respected and admired his talent and his work ethic. Schmidt retired in 1989 and was elected to the Hall of Fame in 1995.

Colorado Rockies

Founded in 1993
0 World Championships
1 NL pennant

The Rockies were an unusual team from the beginning, simply because of where they play. Denver, Colorado, is known as the Mile High City because it is located more than 5,000 feet (about a mile) above sea level. Why is this important? At high altitudes, breaking balls don't curve very much, which makes them easier to hit, and batted balls fly farther. For the first nine years of the team's existence, Rockies home games were nearly always slugfests. From 1995 to 2001, Coors Field saw an average of 13.8 runs and 3.2 home runs *per game*! Since 2002, the Rockies have stored their baseballs

in a specially made humidor that cost $15,000. The humidor controls temperature and humidity so the balls won't be damaged by Denver's low humidity, and run scoring at Coors has gone way down.

Through their first decade, the Rockies focused on finding the best sluggers. The "Blake Street Bombers," led by Andrés Galarraga, put the Rockies in the playoffs in 1995. More recently, the team has developed some excellent pitchers. They made their second playoff appearance ever in 2007 after winning 14 of their last 15 regular season games. They made it to the World Series but were swept by the Boston Red Sox for the championship. The Rockies returned to the playoffs in 2009, but they lost in the first round.

St. Louis Cardinals

Founded in 1882
Other names: St. Louis Brown Stockings, St. Louis Browns, St. Louis Perfectos
11 World Championships (1926, 1931, 1934, 1942, 1944, 1946, 1964, 1967, 1982, 2006, 2011)
19 NL pennants

The Cardinals' 11 World Series titles are the most in National League history, and second overall behind the Yankees. But the Cardinals' beginnings were modest. Founded as the St. Louis Brown Stockings, they were expelled from the National League after two years for a game-fixing scandal. Entering the American Association as the Browns in 1882, they quickly rose to the top, but the AA disbanded following the 1891 season. Rejoining the NL in 1892, they sank to the bottom of the standings, and remained in that vicinity until 1919.

The revival of the franchise, which changed its name to Cardinals in 1900, began with the arrival of Branch Rickey.

Gold Glove: Each year the best fielder at each position in both the National and American Leagues is given the Gold Glove award for fielding excellence.

As business manager, the former catcher started the practice of buying minor-league clubs to serve as farm teams. Players promoted from that system served as the core of the team that lifted the Cardinals to their first World Championship in 1926, and to five more over the next 20 years. Boasting such great players as Joe Medwick, Dizzy Dean, and Stan "The Man" Musial, whose statue stands outside Busch Stadium, the Cardinals won nine pennants, and suffered only three losing seasons between 1921 and 1946.

In the past 30 years, the franchise has been similarly successful, if not as consistent. Whitey Herzog managed the Cardinals to three World Series appearances in the 1980s, with the team built for speed on the artificial turf of the old multipurpose Busch Stadium. Taking over as manager in 1996, Tony La Russa led the team to the playoffs in nine of his 16 seasons, including World Championships in 2006 and 2011, both in the new retro-styled Busch Stadium.

Famous Cardinal: Ozzie Smith, 1978–1996

HR	RBI	AVG
28	793	.262

Just 28 homers in 19 years? How can a player with those kinds of career numbers be one of the all-time best Cardinals? Ozzie Smith represents the other side of the game: defense. He was called the "Wizard of Oz" because no one had ever played shortstop like Ozzie. He could get to groundballs that no one else could reach, often diving in either direction before somehow making the throw to first base for the out. He also turned more double plays than any player in history.

Ozzie dazzled the fans and frustrated the opponents who thought they had a hit until he turned it into an out. He won a

Ozzie Smith

Ozzie Smith was so excited about starting a game, he would do a flip in the first inning as he ran out to his position.

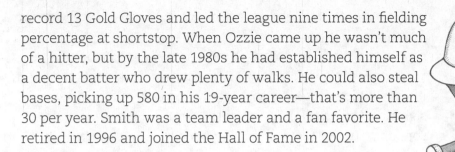

record 13 Gold Gloves and led the league nine times in fielding percentage at shortstop. When Ozzie came up he wasn't much of a hitter, but by the late 1980s he had established himself as a decent batter who drew plenty of walks. He could also steal bases, picking up 580 in his 19-year career—that's more than 30 per year. Smith was a team leader and a fan favorite. He retired in 1996 and joined the Hall of Fame in 2002.

Miami Marlins

Founded in 1993
Other Names: Florida Marlins
2 World Championships (1997, 2003)
2 NL pennants

Even though they have been around only since 1993, the Marlins have already won two World Championships. For the first, in 1997, the team signed many star players that earned big salaries. Despite their World Series victory over the Cleveland Indians, the Marlins failed to attract sufficiently large crowds to the converted football stadium where they played, and the owner decided he couldn't afford to keep paying his stars. So he held a fire sale, trading most of his best players. That left the Marlins among the worst teams in baseball, and they didn't manage another winning season until 2003.

The good news was that several of the young players acquired in those drastic trades and in the annual amateur draft matured and, under the skillful direction of 72-year-old Jack McKeon, surged to surprising victories over the Giants and Cubs in the 2003 NL playoffs and the Yankees in the World Series, capped by Josh Beckett's complete-game shutout in Game 6 at Yankee Stadium. Later, the Marlins,

WORDS to KNOW

The Cy Young Award: The Cy Young Award, named after the pitcher with the most wins in baseball history, is given each year to the best pitcher in each league.

The Big Unit Is Scary!

Randy Johnson, the 6'10" lefty known as the "Big Unit" has won five Cy Young Awards. In the 1993 All-Star Game, the Phillies' best hitter, lefthander John Kruk, stepped up against Randy Johnson for the first time. Kruk was completely intimidated. He ducked and backed away from three straight pitches even though all three were strikes.

under different ownership, again chose to break up the team for financial reasons.

On the verge of moving into their new baseball-only park with a retractable roof in 2012, the Marlins reversed recent history by loading their roster with expensive free-agent signings. However, they stumbled through a last-place season, and cut the team payroll by more than 60 percent in time for the 2013 campaign.

Arizona Diamondbacks

Founded in 1998
1 World Championship (2001)
1 NL pennant

Although the Diamondbacks are the youngest National League team, they reached the playoffs in five of their first 15 seasons, and won a dramatic seven-game World Series against the defending champion Yankees in 2001. They also experienced four last-place finishes in the NL West before returning to contention under manager Kirk Gibson.

The Diamondbacks play in Chase Field, a big, quirky ballpark with a retractable roof and a pool behind the right-field fence to combat the desert heat. The center field fence is tall and very deep. The team has always put outstanding pitchers on the mound, taking advantage of the large field. Curt Schilling and Randy Johnson were co-MVPs of the 2001 World Series; Brandon Webb was among the top pitchers of the decade. Gibson drove the D-backs, as they are known in Phoenix, back into the playoffs in 2011, and they have remained a contender behind the hitting of powerful first baseman Paul Goldschmidt.

New York Mets

Founded in 1962
2 World Championships (1969, 1986)
4 NL pennants

After both the Dodgers and Giants left New York for California after the 1957 season, National League fans wanted a replacement team. They didn't want to root for the hated Yankees, the only remaining New York team. So the Mets, adopting the colors of the departing franchises—blue for the Dodgers and orange for the Giants—were formed as an expansion team in 1962.

In their first season, the Mets were genuinely awful, compiling a 40-120 record. However, because they featured some of the Dodgers' and Giants' old heroes, and because the beloved and entertaining manager Casey Stengel managed them, they were embraced by the fans. After seven years of dismal finishes, just as New York was growing impatient with the results, the Mets suddenly blossomed in the midst of the 1969 season. Behind the standout pitching of Tom Seaver and Jerry Koosman, and under the even-handed direction of manager Gil Hodges (an original Met), the team rallied to overcome the heavily favored Cubs in the first year of division play, sweep the Braves in the NLCS, and stun a great Baltimore Orioles team for a World Championship that was deemed a miracle.

The sudden death of Hodges in the spring of 1972 cast a pall over the franchise, although the Mets did squeeze out a second World Series appearance in 1973, despite the worst record (82-79) of any team to qualify for the Fall Classic. It would be more than a decade before they made it back, riding the arm of Dwight Gooden, the leadership of Keith

WORDS to KNOW

expansion team: Since 1962, the National League has added seven entirely new teams—not teams that moved from city to city or from league to league, but teams that were created from scratch. These teams are called "expansion" teams. They get their players by drafting from the existing teams. Expansion teams usually aren't very good for their first few years, but the Arizona Diamondbacks are a well-known exception.

Hernandez and Gary Carter, and a favorable bounce to a memorable World Championship in 1986.

Mike Piazza led the team to the first Subway Series in 44 years, a losing showdown against the Yankees, in 2000. However, historic collapses cost the Mets the pennant in 2007 and a playoff berth on the last day of the season in 2008, after which not even a move from Shea Stadium to sparkling Citi Field in 2009 could prevent a decline.

Famous Met: Tom Seaver, 1967–1986

W-L	ERA	K
311-205	2.86	3,640

When "Tom Terrific" came up with the New York Mets in 1967, the Mets were the worst team in the major leagues. By 1969, they shocked everyone and won 100 games, with Tom Seaver winning 25 of them on the way to a World Championship. Seaver won his first of three Cy Young Awards that year and became the heart and soul of the Mets. In 1973 he led the Mets back to the World Series, but this time they lost to the A's. Much to the disappointment of Mets fans, he was traded away in 1977, returning only for a brief stint before his retirement in 1986. In his career, he won 20 or more games four times and led the league in strikeouts five times. Seaver retired as one of the 20 winningest pitchers of all time, and he sits sixth all-time in strikeouts. He was elected to the Hall of Fame in 1992 and even after that returned to the Mets one more time—only this time as an announcer.

Play Ball

A baseball player must be sure to follow the rules of the game, or he could get sent to the dugout! You must carefully follow the directions below to learn the words that finish the following popular saying: "Some people say that playing baseball is as American as eating _____."

1. Print the word BASEBALL.   BASEBALL

_____

2. Switch the position of
   the first two letters.

_____

3. Move the 5th letter between
   the 2nd and 3rd letters.

_____

4. Switch the positions of
   the 4th and 8th letters.

_____

5. Change the 6th letter to P.

_____

6. Change the last letter to E.

_____

7. Change both B s to P s.

_____

8. Change the 7th letter to I.

Atlanta Braves

Founded in 1876
Other names: Boston Red Caps, Boston Beaneaters, Boston Doves, Boston Rustlers, Boston Bees, Boston Braves, Milwaukee Braves
3 World Championships (1914, 1957, 1995)
17 NL pennants

The only franchise to win a World Championship in three different cities, the Braves started out in Boston a long time ago. They were very, very good in the nineteenth century, winning eight NL pennants between 1876 and 1899. They won the World Series in 1914, but weren't contenders again until the late 1940s.

The team moved to Milwaukee in 1953, and then became the first major-league team to represent the South in 1966. The Braves were the joke of the National League through much of the 1970s and 1980s. However, in 1990, the team hired general manager John Schuerholz away from Kansas City. Schuerholz signed Bobby Cox as his manager, and Cox named Leo Mazzone his pitching coach. Under their leadership, the Braves dominated the National League in the 1990s. With phenomenal starting pitching, they won their division every year between 1991 and 2005, wresting the World Series title in 1995 from the Cleveland Indians.

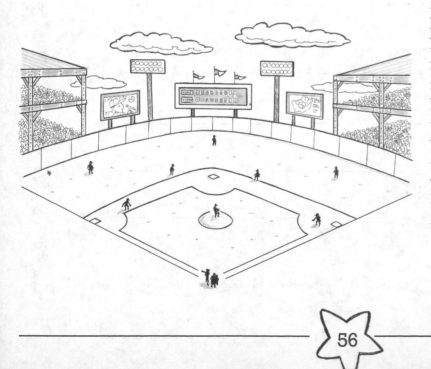

Famous Brave: Hank Aaron, 1954–1976

HR	RBI	AVG
755	2,297	.305

Many people thought Babe Ruth's record of 714 career home runs would never be broken. Hank Aaron, nicknamed "the Hammer," knew better. Aaron played briefly in the Negro Leagues before being signed in 1954 by the Milwaukee Braves, who moved to Atlanta in 1966.

Aaron never topped 50 homers in a season, but he belted at least 25 home runs 18 times, with a high of 47. He also posted more than 120 RBIs seven times while setting the all-time career RBI record. By the time he finished his 23-year career back in Milwaukee as a member of the Brewers, he was also near the top in games played, hits, runs scored, and doubles. Aaron made the Hall of Fame in 1982.

Mazzone on Pitching

Most starting pitchers are afraid to throw too much between starts for fear of hurting their arm. Braves pitching coach Leo Mazzone thought that was ridiculous. He had his pitchers throw off the mound twice between starts, though only at about half speed. He seemed to know what he was doing because the Braves had the best starting pitching in the majors for more than a decade.

Famous Brave: Greg Maddux, 1986–2008

W-L	ERA	K
355-227	3.16	3,371

He didn't have the blazing fastball of Randy Johnson, and he didn't put up amazing strikeout totals, but his secret to pitching was, as he put it, "making your strikes look like balls and your balls look like strikes." Greg Maddux was a very smart pitcher with tremendous control who knew how to get batters out. In 1997, for example, he walked only 14 batters in over 230 innings. He knew how to throw several pitches very well, and he could hit the corners of the plate with all of them. In 1995 and 1996, with the Braves, Greg went a combined 35-8 with a 1.60 ERA,

capturing two of his four Cy Young Awards; in fact, some people in the late 1990s joked about renaming the award the "Greg Maddux Award."

San Diego Padres

Founded in 1969	
0 World Championships	
2 NL pennants	

The expansion Padres posted only one winning record over their first 15 seasons. However, not only did they win 92 games in 1984, they also won their division and the pennant, rallying behind young Tony Gwynn and veteran Steve Garvey to overcome a 2-0 deficit in the best-of-five NLCS against the Cubs. They staged a similar rise in 1998, propelled once again by Gwynn, then 38 and an eight-time batting champion. On both occasions, the Padres were overwhelmed in the World Series, first by the Tigers and then the Yankees, winning a combined total of one game.

Bruce Bochy, the backup catcher on the 1984 Padres, managed the team in 1998. He also managed the club in the other three years in which it qualified for the playoffs—1996, 2005, and 2006. He left in 2007 to manage the Giants, who won the World Series in 2010 and 2012. The Padres, who moved into dazzling Petco Park in 2004, have been in a rebuilding mode in recent years.

Brothers Who Hit Home Runs

There have been many brothers who played major league baseball, from Joe and Dom DiMaggio to Cal and Billy Ripken to Aaron and Bret Boone. But who were the brothers who hit the most combined home runs? Hank and Tommie Aaron. Hammerin' Hank hit 755, while Tommie added on 13 for a grand total of 768.

Famous Padre: Tony Gwynn, 1982–2001

HR	RBI	AVG
135	1,138	.338

From the moment he came up to the big leagues, Gwynn was the best hitter in baseball and one of the best of all time. His career .338 average is up there with the greats of the early 1900s, and in 1994 he came within 6 points of batting .400, something that hadn't been done since 1941. Gwynn led the league in batting seven times, hitting over .360 four times. He could hit any pitch for a single or double and hardly ever struck out, which helps explain why he had over 3,000 career hits. In his younger years he was also a great base stealer and tremendous defensive player. Gwynn retired at the end of the 2001 season after 20 years with the San Diego Padres and 19 consecutive .300 seasons. He was inducted into the Hall of Fame in 2007. His son, Tony Gwynn Jr., played two seasons for the Padres.

Cincinnati Reds

Founded in 1882
Other Names: Cincinnati Red Stockings, Cincinnati Redlegs
5 World Championships (1919, 1940, 1975, 1976, 1990)
10 NL pennants

The original Cincinnati Red Stockings team was formed in 1863. Five years later, they became the first professional baseball team, composed entirely of players paid a salary by the team owner. That team lasted until 1870. A new Cincinnati Red Stockings team joined the National League in

1876 but was kicked out of the league. So today's Reds are really the third team to represent Cincinnati in professional baseball.

The Reds' first World Championship, in 1919, was clouded by the "Black Sox" scandal, in which gamblers paid members of the Chicago White Sox to lose the World Series. The most famous Reds teams dominated the 1970s, when they were known as the "Big Red Machine." Johnny Bench, Pete Rose, Joe Morgan, Tony Perez, and George Foster formed the core of a fearsome batting order for manager Sparky Anderson. From 1961 to 1981, the Reds reeled off 19 winning seasons and seven playoff appearances.

After a few tough seasons at the start of the 1980s, the Reds improved under the direction of hometown hero Pete Rose. He was relieved as manager in 1989 after acknowledging that he bet on baseball games and was followed by Lou Piniella, who led the Reds to a World Series sweep of the defending champion Oakland A's in 1990. The Reds have become perennial playoff contenders again under manager Dusty Baker, largely through the offensive efforts of Joey Votto and Brandon Phillips.

Famous Red: Johnny Bench, 1967–1983

HR	RBI	AVG
389	1,376	.267

There was never a greater major-league catcher than Johnny Bench. He broke into the major leagues in style when he was just 20 years old, making the All-Star Game and winning Rookie of the Year honors. In 1970, his third season, Bench won the National League MVP with 45 homers and 148 RBIs while leading the Reds to the World Series. Bench

topped the 100 RBI mark on five occasions and was the main cog in Cincinnati's "Big Red Machine."

Besides his tremendous power hitting and many clutch hits, Bench was also an incredible defensive catcher and was known for his great throwing arm. He won 10 Gold Glove awards as the best defensive catcher in the National League until injuries forced him to spend more time at third and first base. Two World Championships and consistently good play made Johnny Bench one of baseball's most popular players of the 1970s. But the injuries from catching caught up with him, and by age 35 Bench had to call it quits. He was elected to the Hall of Fame in 1985.

WORDS to KNOW

player-manager: Occasionally the manager of a team is also a player, referred to as the player-manager. Hiring a player to manage the team used to be more common than it is now. The only player-manager in the last few decades was Pete Rose, who played for and managed the Reds in 1985 and 1986.

Los Angeles Dodgers

Founded in 1884
Other Names (all from their Brooklyn Days): Brooklyn Atlantics, Grays, Grooms, Bridegrooms, Superbas, Robins, and Dodgers
6 World Championships (1955, 1959, 1963, 1965, 1981, 1988)
21 NL pennants

While the Dodgers occupied their original home of Brooklyn, New York, they made it to the World Series nine times—the last seven against the New York Yankees—but won only in 1955. Just two years after their lone championship, Brooklyn fans were heartbroken to see their "Bums," as they were fondly called, move thousands of miles away to Los Angeles.

But southern California embraced its new team, and the Dodgers won a World Series in only their second season on the West Coast, in 1959. After four years in the misshapen Los Angeles Memorial Coliseum, they moved into a beautiful new stadium in 1962, and reached the World Series in three of the next four years.

The Dodgers have historically been one of the best-run clubs in baseball. Great pitchers have been at the heart of the team's success, from Hall of Famers Sandy Koufax and Don Drysdale in the 1960s, to Fernando Valenzuela and Orel Hershiser in the 1980s, when Los Angeles won the last two of its six championships. The stability of the Dodgers became a major issue for baseball when Frank McCourt and his wife, who had purchased the franchise in 2004, divorced, and the team sought bankruptcy protection. After a brief takeover by Major League Baseball, McCourt was persuaded to sell in 2012 to a group that included former Lakers' basketball star Magic Johnson for $2 billion, a record sum for a professional sports team.

The Beloved Bums from Brooklyn

Many people used to get around New York City by taking the trolley, which was a sort of train that ran at street level. People had to dodge the trolleys as they crossed streets—hence, the baseball team became the Brooklyn Trolley Dodgers. But fans sometimes referred to their team simply as the "Bums."

Famous Dodger: Jackie Robinson, 1947–1956

HR	RBI	AVG
137	734	.311

Jackie Robinson broke into the major leagues with the Brooklyn Dodgers in 1947 at the age of 28 after several years in the Negro Leagues and two years in the minors. He led the league in stolen bases and won Rookie of the Year honors. But his entry into the majors was far more significant than his stats. Robinson broke the color barrier, becoming the first black player to play in the major leagues, at least since the late 1800s. Making a major statement for his race wasn't new to Robinson, who had been court-martialed out of the United States Army after he had refused to sit in the back of a bus because of the color of his skin.

The early days of his career were very difficult. Fans, players on other teams, and even many of his own teammates were cruel. Some players even started a petition that said they would not play in the game with him. But there

were a lot of people on his side. He got support from some of his teammates, the Dodgers manager and front office, and even the baseball commissioner. He also had the support and hopes of African Americans, who rooted passionately for him—even if he was playing against their own team! He also showed a great deal of sheer determination and proved himself as a first-rate ballplayer.

In 1949 Robinson hit .342, which led the league in batting, and he was named the MVP. In the next 10 years he would make a huge breakthrough for the game of baseball. Robinson's legacy continued long after his seven World Series appearances or his induction into the Hall of Fame in 1962. In 1997, stadiums all over the country honored the 50-year anniversary of Robinson's achievement. His uniform number, 42, was retired throughout major-league baseball.

Switch Hitter

Can you see the 10 differences between the two pictures of this batter?

HINT: It doesn't count that he's facing in different directions— that's what a switch hitter does!

Hall of Fame Designated Hitter

Brewer Paul Molitor hit for a lifetime average of .306. He played most of his career in Milwaukee, leading the team to its only World Series appearance in 1982. He was elected to the Hall of Fame in 2004. Since the Brewers usually used him as a designated hitter, that's the position on his plaque—the only player in the Hall as a DH.

Though Jackie Robinson will be remembered foremost for breaking baseball's color barrier, it must be noted that his performance earned him recognition as one of the all-time greatest players of any color.

Milwaukee Brewers

Founded in 1969
Other names: Seattle Pilots
0 World Championships
1 AL pennant (1982); 0 NL pennants

In 1969, the American League granted membership to two expansion teams, the Kansas City Royals and the Seattle Pilots. The Pilots, playing their first season in a minor-league ballpark, went bankrupt. They were sold to Bud Selig, a Milwaukee car dealer who had been a minor shareholder in the Braves before they left town for Atlanta. He renamed them the Brewers, and controlled the franchise until he was appointed commissioner of baseball in 1992.

The Brewers were rarely contenders in the AL, nor in the National League, after they switched to it after the 1997 season. They did make the playoffs in the split season of 1981, and represented the AL in the 1982 World Series with a team of sluggers branded "Harvey's Wallbangers" in honor of manager Harvey Kuenn. However, their next postseason appearance didn't occur until 2008. With a team featuring Prince Fielder and Most Valuable Player Ryan Braun, they won their first NL division series and first NL playoff series in 2011 before falling to the Cardinals in the NLCS.

Pittsburgh Pirates

Founded in 1892
Other Names: Pittsburgh Alleghenys
5 World Championships (1909, 1925, 1960, 1971, 1979)
9 NL pennants

The Pirates reached their peak in the 1970s, when they rivaled the Cincinnati Big Red Machine as the team of the decade. While the franchise shifted from historic Forbes Field to Three Rivers Stadium, and leadership passed from the late, great Roberto Clemente to slugger Willie Stargell, the Pirates made six appearances in the playoffs. They won the World Series in 1971, with Clemente in a starring role, and in 1979, with Stargell overseeing a joyous group that chose the disco hit "We Are Family" as its theme song.

It was a decade before the Pirates returned to the playoffs. A young Barry Bonds led Pittsburgh to the National League Championship Series in three consecutive years, but the Pirates' hopes came crashing down in Game 7 of the 1992 series, when the Braves scored three runs in the bottom of the ninth inning to clinch a second straight National League pennant. Bonds' throw to the plate was just late as Sid Bream slid across with the winning run on Francisco Cabrera's single.

Bonds left for San Francisco as a free agent the following season, and the Pirates slipped into oblivion. The only positive development in the next 20 years was the opening of beautiful PNC Park, facing the Allegheny River and the city's skyscrapers, in 2001. However, the patient hand of manager Clint Hurdle paid off in 2013, when young stars Andrew McCutchen and Pedro Alvarez led the team to the playoffs.

Who's Who?

Some baseball nicknames are easy to guess. For example, almost all players who have had the last name "Rhodes" have gotten the nickname "Dusty." See how many of the famous nicknames on the left you can match with the real names on the right. Put the number of the correct nickname on the line in front of each real name.

1. The Big Train
2. Tom Terrific
3. Cyclone
4. Joltin' Joe
5. Double X
6. Mr. October
7. The Mick
8. Say Hey Kid
9. Stan The Man
10. Charlie Hustle
11. Wizard of Oz
12. The Big Unit
13. The Rocket

___ Cy Young
___ Jimmy Foxx
___ Joe DiMaggio
___ Mickey Mantle
___ Ozzie Smith
___ Pete Rose
___ Randy Johnson
___ Reggie Jackson
___ Roger Clemens
___ Stan Musial
___ Tom Seaver
___ Walter Johnson
___ Willie Mays

Look! It's "Bubbles" MacCoy!

Famous Pirate: Roberto Clemente, 1955–1972

HR	RBI	AVG
240	1,305	.317

Roberto Clemente was a tremendous all-around ballplayer. Not only could he hit for a high average, but he had power and was a super defensive outfielder, winning 12 Gold Gloves. He joined the Pirates in the mid-1950s as a 20-year-old rookie from Puerto Rico. He went on to become the greatest player from Puerto Rico and the first Hispanic player elected to the Hall of Fame. Clemente led the National League in batting four times in the 1960s, and four times he had more than 200 hits in a season. He appeared in two World Series for the Pirates and batted .362 overall, helping lead the Pirates to the title in 1971.

Clemente became one of the few players to get his 3,000th hit, which came at the end of the 1972 season. It would be his last hit ever. On New Year's Eve of that year he was on his way to deliver supplies to victims of a severe earthquake in Nicaragua when the plane he was on crashed. Clemente died at age 38 but is remembered as a hero both on and off the field.

Washington Nationals

Founded in 1969
Other Names: Montreal Expos
0 World Championships
0 NL pennants

The Nationals still await their first appearance in a World Series 45 years after the franchise began play in Montreal. However, they are a lot closer than they've been in years, thanks to a roster of good young players headlined by

FUN FACT

Stephen Strasburg

In recent years, young pitchers have been limited to a set number of innings in order to prevent arm injuries. However, the Washington Nationals set off a nationwide debate in 2012 when they announced that young star Stephen Strasburg would be limited to 160 innings, despite the team's involvement in a division race. Strasburg, who had a 15-6 record, made his final pitch of the season on September 8. Although the Nationals won their division without him, they faltered in their first playoff series without their ace.

outfielder Bryce Harper, and pitchers Stephen Strasburg and Gio Gonzalez. The trio led the 2012 team to its first winning season and first division title since moving south in 2005.

While in Canada, the team, then known as the Expos, developed outstanding talent—Rusty Staub, Tim Raines, Vladimir Guerrero, Andre Dawson, Larry Walker, Pedro Martinez, Moisés Alou, and Andrés Galarraga, as well as Hall of Fame catcher Gary Carter—but reaped little reward. The Expos' luck was so bad that when a players' strike closed down the major leagues in 1994, cancelling the World Series, Montreal sported a 74-40 record, the best in baseball. The Expos' only playoff appearance occurred in 1981, another strike season, which was split in two. Montreal qualified by winning the second-half race, defeated the Phillies in five games, and then lost a heartbreaking five-game NLCS to the Dodgers.

Chicago Cubs

Founded in 1876
Other Names: Chicago White Stockings, Chicago Colts, Chicago Orphans
2 World Championships (1907, 1908)
16 NL pennants

The Cubs were the best team in the National League in the first decade of the twentieth century, advancing to four World Series in a five-year period, beating the Detroit Tigers in both 1907 and 1908 with a combined loss of only one game. They got back to the World Series in six more seasons, including 1945, when they fell to the Tigers in seven games and, apparently, suffered the Curse of the Billy Goat.

According to legend, Billy Sianis, the owner of the Billy Goat Tavern in Chicago, brought his bar's mascot to the World Series at Wrigley Field. The goat was not permitted to enter

FUN FACT

Wrigley Field

The Cubs started playing at Wrigley in 1916. Since then, Wrigley Field has become more than just a ballpark; it's a landmark in Chicago. The ivy-covered brick outfield walls, an old hand-operated scoreboard, and rooftop views from the surrounding apartment buildings all add to the unique atmosphere of the most popular park in the National League. Until 1988, all games at Wrigley were day games. Even now, the Cubs play more day games than any other team.

because, he was told, it smelled. Sianis was so angry, that he cursed the team, saying, "Them Cubs, they ain't gonna win no more!"

He was right. After losing that Series, the Cubs didn't even qualify for the playoffs for the next 38 years. They led, 3-0, in the deciding game of the 1984 NLCS before a ground ball went through an infielder's legs, and they lost in San Diego. What happened in 2003 was even worse. They held a 3-0 lead in the eighth inning of the game that could send them to the World Series, but a Cubs fan interfered with a foul fly ball just above Chicago left fielder Moisés Alou (preventing him from catching it), and then the shortstop let a ground ball through his legs. The Cubs lost that game, and the following game to the Marlins. The team's failure to win a championship since 1908 is the longest in American professional sports.

Mr. Cub: Ernie Banks, 1953–1971

HR	RBI	AVG
512	1,636	.274

Ernie Banks began his career in the Negro Leagues in 1950. He joined the Cubs as their shortstop in 1953. Banks was known for his deep love of the game, particularly where the Cubs were involved. It was Banks who first called Wrigley Field the "Friendly Confines," a nickname for the ballpark that's used regularly even today. In 1982, the Cubs retired Banks's number 14—the first number they had ever retired. A bronze statue of Ernie Banks stands outside Wrigley Field in honor of the man called "Mr. Cub."

Famous Fungo!

Can you match the silly answers to the funny riddles?

1. What do you call a baseball player who only hits flap-jacks?

2. What do you call a baseball player who throws dairy products?

3. What do you call a dog that stands behind home plate?

____ A milk pitcher!

____ A catcher's mutt!

____ A pancake batter!

A "fungo" is actually a ball hit to the infield during fielding practice. Fungoes are hit with a special thin, light bat called a "fungo stick"!

Chapter 4
The American League

The American League

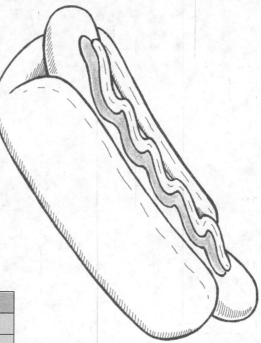

The American League is sometimes called the "junior circuit," while the National League is the "senior circuit." Why? Because the AL was formed 25 years after the NL. Of course, the AL has still been around for as long as anyone can remember. It began in 1901 when the old Western League chose a new name, and decided that they were just as much a major league as the NL.

There were eight teams in the original American League. All eight teams are still around, though only the Tigers are still in the same city with the same name.

The Original 1901 American League

1901 Team Name	Modern Team Name
Chicago White Stockings	Chicago White Sox
Boston Americans	Boston Red Sox
Detroit Tigers	Detroit Tigers
Philadelphia Athletics	Oakland Athletics
Baltimore Orioles	New York Yankees
Washington Senators	Minnesota Twins
Cleveland Blues	Cleveland Indians
Milwaukee Brewers	Baltimore Orioles

Fifteen teams make up the American League today. The only major difference between an AL team and an NL team is the use of the designated hitter. Pitchers don't bat in games played in AL ballparks. The AL has enjoyed a significant advantage over the NL in this century, both in the results of all-star games and interleague play. However, World Series success has been split almost evenly during the same period.

Texas Rangers

Founded in 1961
Other Names: Washington Senators
0 World Championships
2 AL pennants

When the Washington Senators moved into a former minor-league ballpark in Arlington, Texas, in 1972, their only significant possessions were aged slugger Frank Howard and manager Ted Williams, one of the greatest hitters in baseball history. Howard was traded during the season and Williams resigned afterward. Their most notable accomplishments in the next 25 years were an ownership group that included a future Texas governor and U.S. president, George W. Bush, as well as the construction of a new ballpark in 1994.

Not until 1996 did the Rangers qualify for the playoffs, and they lost their first three postseason series, all to the Yankees, in 1996, 1998, and 1999. They reacted to a losing season in 2000 by signing Alex Rodriguez to a staggering 10-year, $252 million contract. He was traded after three seasons in which his salary forced the Rangers to deplete their overall roster, particularly on the pitching side. They finally put together another playoff team after Ron Washington became manager and Hall of Fame pitcher Nolan Ryan rejoined the franchise as president.

Led by Most Valuable Player Josh Hamilton, infielder Michael Young, and rookie closer Neftalí Feliz, the Rangers reached the World Series in 2010. They enjoyed their best season the following year, when they returned to the World Series, and came within a strike of a World Championship in both the ninth and 10th innings of Game 6, before being denied by the Cardinals. Feliz underwent surgery in 2012, after which Young was traded and Hamilton left as a free agent. However, the Rangers remain a contender in the AL West.

Famous Ranger: Nolan Ryan, 1966–1993

W-L	ERA	K
324-292	3.19	5,386

Nolan Ryan was truly a flame-thrower, firing the ball harder and faster than anyone had ever seen. When Ryan came up with the Mets in 1966 he could throw very hard, but he had control problems and walked a lot of hitters. In 1972, the Mets traded him to the California Angels, and there he turned into a big winner and became the king of strikeouts. He led the league 11 times in strikeouts, and in 1973, he struck out a whopping 383 hitters. While most

WORDS to KNOW

no-hitter: When a pitcher allows no hits in a game, it's called a no-hitter. It's still a no-hitter if the pitcher walks batters or if batters reach base on fielding errors. In fact, it's possible for a pitcher to pitch a no-hitter but still lose the game!

Hink Pinks

The answer to Hink Pinks are two rhyming words. Both words of the answer should have the same number of syllables. See if you can score four!

1. The heavier of two batters.

F _ _ _ _ _   B _ _ _ _ _

2. Where you throw a bad referee.

U _ _ D _ _ _

3. Nine baseball players shouting at once.

T _ _ _ S _ _ _ _

4. The last part of a baseball game when one team has more points.

W _ _ _ _ _ _   I _ _ _ _ _

pitchers would be thrilled to throw one no-hitter in their careers, Ryan threw seven—a major-league record.

A native of Texas, Ryan was excited when he got to play for the Houston Astros, where he topped Walter Johnson's long-held all-time career strikeout record in 1983 at the age of 36. Ryan, however, was far from done. Somehow, no matter how hard he threw, his arm never seemed to get tired. He surprised everyone by pitching in the big leagues for another 10 years, including several with the Rangers, until he finally retired at age 46. By that time he had over 5,000 strikeouts, far more than anyone else. He made the Hall of Fame in 1999—his Hall of Fame picture includes a Rangers cap.

New York Yankees

Founded in 1901
Other names: Baltimore Orioles, New York Highlanders
27 World Championships (1923, 1927, 1928, 1932, 1936, 1937, 1938, 1939, 1941, 1943, 1947, 1949, 1950, 1951, 1952, 1953, 1956, 1958, 1961, 1962, 1977, 1978, 1996, 1998, 1999, 2000, 2009)
40 AL pennants

The Yankees are the most successful major-league team. They are the best-known team nationally—and even worldwide. They have been so good so often—since brewery owner Jacob Ruppert bought the club in 1915, and purchased the contract of Babe Ruth five years later—that it's easier to list the few times they *haven't* reached the postseason: 1965–74 and 1982–94 represent their longest times out of the playoffs since 1921. In their most recent dynasty, under manager Joe Torre, the Yankees won the World Series in four of five years between 1996 and 2000.

Although they reached the postseason 11 times in the next 12 years, some fans expressed disappointment with the Yankees, because they won only one World Series, in 2009, under Torre's successor, Joe Girardi. Yes, the Yankees have had expectations of a World Series victory every year since a partnership led by George Steinbrenner bought the franchise in 1973 from CBS. Known as the Boss, Steinbrenner expanded the brand, raised the payroll to the largest in baseball, formed his own television network, and built a new Yankee Stadium before his death.

Many of the game's greatest players, starting with Ruth, have worn the Yankee pinstripes. Ruth teamed with Lou Gehrig to produce the first Yankee dynasty in the 1920s. Joe DiMaggio followed in the 1930s and 1940s, only to be replaced by Mickey Mantle in the 1950s. Roger Maris hit 61 home runs in 1961, to surpass Ruth's record of 60 in 1927. In the 1970s, Reggie Jackson became known as "Mr. October" for his postseason heroics. The great first baseman Don Mattingly joined the team in 1982, and retired in 1995 after only one playoff series, the last lean period in club history. Derek Jeter, the captain who missed much of the 2013 season with an injury suffered in the 2012 playoffs, is the best known and most loved of the current Yankees, the shortstop on five championship teams.

Famous Yankee: Babe Ruth, 1914–1935

HR	RBI	AVG	W-L	ERA	K
714	2,213	.342	94-46	2.28	488

It's almost impossible to find anyone who hasn't heard of "the Babe." Also nicknamed the Bambino, George Herman "Babe" Ruth could do it all. He began as a pitcher with the Boston Red Sox before moving to the outfield. He went

on to change the face of baseball. When Ruth led the major leagues with 29 home runs in 1919, it was the first time a player had hit more than 25 in a season. He was traded to the Yankees, where he became the greatest home run hitter ever.

Ruth's 714 home runs stood as the record until Hank Aaron passed that mark in 1974. Had Ruth not been a pitcher for several years, who knows how many he would have hit. He led the league in home runs (or tied for the lead) 12 times. He also batted .342 for his career and is still considered by most baseball historians as the greatest baseball player ever. Ruth led the Yankees to one World Series title after another.

An often-told story says that in one World Series against the Cubs, Ruth stepped up to the plate, pointed to the bleachers where he was going to hit a home run . . . and then did just that.

Beyond baseball, Ruth was an enormously popular celebrity and was treated like royalty. The Babe enjoyed all the publicity and excitement that surrounded him. It was said that "as he moved, center stage moved with him." Ruth retired in 1935 and was one of the first five players elected to the Hall of Fame in 1939.

Pride of the Yankees

The movie *Pride of the Yankees* is a marvelous, deeply touching story of Gehrig's life.

Famous Yankee: Lou Gehrig, 1923–1939

HR	RBI	AVG
493	1,995	.340

Gehrig was called the Iron Horse because he was always in the lineup. He batted right after the Babe in the great

Yankees lineup and played in Ruth's shadow. Nonetheless, Gehrig was as awesome a hitter as anyone. For 14 consecutive years he drove in more than 100 runs, topping 170 three times and setting an American League record with 184 in 1931. He could do it all. He got more than 200 hits eight times, hit 40 home runs five times, and batted over .300 for 13 consecutive years. His 23 grand slam home runs is the all-time high.

Despite all of his amazing accomplishments, Gehrig is best known for two things. He began a streak in 1925 where he played every single game until 1939, or 2,130 consecutive games, a record most people thought would never be broken. (Cal Ripken Jr. has since topped that incredible record.) Unfortunately, the other thing Gehrig is best remembered for is the reason he removed himself from the lineup eight games into the 1939 season. Gehrig had been suffering from an unknown disease, which later became known as Lou Gehrig's disease. He retired from baseball in May 1939, and in July he famously described himself as the "luckiest man on earth" for the opportunity to have played for the Yankees, and to have been loved by the fans and by his wife. Less than two years later he died at the age of 37. He was elected into the Hall of Fame in 1939.

Tampa Bay Rays

Founded in 1998
Other Names: Tampa Bay Devil Rays
0 World Championships
1 AL pennant

Despite one of the lowest payrolls in the major leagues, the Rays have enjoyed remarkable success since 2008, when

FUN FACT

What's a Devil Ray, Anyway?

The Devil Rays were named after a strange sort of fish that looks more like a flying squirrel than a fish. In 2007, the team decided that they shouldn't be named after a fish. Now the "Rays" refer to rays of light.

they shot from last to first in the American League, facing the Phillies in the World Series. Hampered by an unloved domed stadium in sun-splashed St. Petersburg, Fla., and unable to attract large crowds, they nevertheless qualified for the playoffs on the last day of the seasons in both 2011 and 2013.

Joe Maddon, a former minor-league catcher who spent decades with the Angels organization, has maximized the talent of young players developed in the club's farm system since becoming the Rays' fourth manager in 2006. Pitcher David Price won the American League Cy Young Award in 2012, and third baseman Evan Longoria, the Rookie of the Year in the breakthrough season of 2008, is one of the league's best clutch hitters and most reliable performers.

Baseball Diamond

Can you find six common baseball terms hidden in the diamond grid? Start at a letter and move one space at a time in any direction to a touching letter. You may not use the same letter twice in a word, but you can cross over your own path.

HINT:
One of the terms is an abbreviation!

Boston Red Sox

Founded in 1901
Other Names: Boston Americans, Boston Pilgrims
8 World Championships (1903, 1912, 1915, 1916, 1918, 2004, 2007, 2013)
13 AL pennants

The Red Sox moved into Fenway Park in 1912 and won the World Series four of the next seven years. Pitcher and all-time home run king Babe Ruth was the team's best player and a fan favorite. But in 1919, owner Harry Frazee traded Babe Ruth to the Yankees. Whether as a direct result of that mistake or not, the Red Sox didn't win another World Series for 86 years.

The Sox came close a few times, only to lose in heartbreaking fashion. In 1975, they pushed the Reds to Game 7. In 1978, they lost a one-game playoff to the Yankees on a home run by Bucky Dent. In 1986, a ground ball through Bill Buckner's legs in the sixth game of the World Series allowed the Mets to score the winning run. In 2003, Yankee Bret Boone eliminated the Sox with a walk-off home run in Game 7 of the ALCS. The Red Sox were cursed.

The curse seemed to continue in 2004. The Yankees won the first three games of the ALCS—including a blistering 19-8 victory in Game 3. No team in the history of major-league baseball had ever come back from a 3-0 deficit to win a seven-game series, but the Red Sox beat the odds and took the series. They went on to dispatch the Cardinals in four games to claim the World Championship. The Red Sox have continued to be a dominant power in the AL. They won another World Championship in 2007 and after bottoming out in 2012, they returned to the top of the baseball world in 2013.

WORDS to KNOW

Green Monster: Famous Fenway Park is one of the majors' two ancient ballparks. To make the field fit inside the available space, the left field fence is very, very shallow—about 305 feet. So, to prevent a gazillion home runs to left field, the fence there is 37 feet high. Because the wall is so huge, and because it's painted green, it's called the "Green Monster."

Famous Red Sox: Ted Williams, 1939–1960

HR	RBI	AVG
521	1,839	.344

Ted Williams, known as "the Splendid Splinter," was one of the most remarkable hitters ever. He hit for power, for a high average, and rarely ever struck out. In fact, after his career he wrote a book called *The Science of Hitting*, which is still a terrific book to read for anyone who wants to learn to be a better hitter. As a rookie in 1939, Williams hit .327 and batted .406 in 1941. No one has batted over .400 for an entire season since Williams did it—more than 60 years ago! In 1942, Williams not only led the league in batting average again, but also led with 37 home runs and 137 runs batted in, winning the Triple Crown. Williams's career was interrupted twice, once when he was drafted into the Navy for World War II, and again when he volunteered to serve in the Korean War. Both times he returned to baseball to have great seasons. Williams finally called it quits at age 42 and was inducted into the Hall of Fame in 1965.

Detroit Tigers

Founded in 1901
4 World Championships (1935, 1945, 1968, 1984)
11 AL pennants

The opening of Comerica Park helped to revitalize decaying Detroit starting in 2000, but it wasn't until the arrival of manager Jim Leyland in 2006 that the Tigers emerged from the ruins. Under Leyland, the team enjoyed its first winning season in 13 years—a drought that included 119 losses in 2003—and the Tigers went all the way to the World Series

FUN FACT

30-Game Winner

The last pitcher to top the thirty-win mark was Denny McLain, who won 31 games for the Detroit Tigers in 1968. He's the only pitcher to win more than 30 games in a season in more than 40 years!

before bowing to the Cardinals. Nine years later, led by Miguel Cabrera's Triple Crown hitting, and Justin Verlander's power pitching, they returned to the World Series, only to suffer a sweep by the Giants. The Tigers' consecutive trips to the playoffs in 2011 and 2012 marked the first back-to-back postseason appearances by the club since 1934–1935.

Detroit was among the more formidable teams during the early years of the AL, thanks mostly to the presence of Ty Cobb, perhaps the greatest hitter and most competitive player of his or any other era. In addition to Cobb, the Tigers have been represented by many Hall of Fame players, most notably Mickey Cochrane, Charlie Gehringer, Hank Greenberg, and Al Kaline.

Manager, Too

Cobb not only played for the Tigers, but for six years was a player-manager for them, too, amassing a 479–444 record. He took the Tigers as high as second place in the American League.

Famous Tiger: Ty Cobb, 1905–1928

HR	RBI	AVG
118	1,961	.367

Cobb was one of the toughest players of all time. He worked very hard and spent hours practicing hitting, sliding, and throwing to make it to the major leagues in 1905 at the age of 18. The hard work paid off. Cobb played 24 years, almost all for the Tigers, and hit under .300 just once, as a rookie. He batted over .400 three times and led the league in batting average 12 times on his way to an incredible .367 career batting average. Cobb was also one of the best base stealers ever, stealing nearly 900 bases.

Cobb's hitting made him one of the first five players elected to the Hall of Fame. The fans enjoyed watching Cobb, but he rarely got along with his teammates, and opposing players hated him. He would sharpen his spikes and then slide in hard, feet first. Cobb said that if he had one thing he could do differently it would be to have more friends.

Chicago White Sox

Founded in 1901
3 World Championships (1906, 1917, 2005)
6 AL pennants

Although the White Sox won a World Series as recently as 2005 (almost a century after the last championship claimed by the Cubs), and U.S. Cellular Field is the only modern ballpark in the city, they still trail the Cubs in popularity. Sometimes referred to as the "South Siders," because they play on the south side of the city, they traditionally finish second in attendance to the Cubs and their ancient "shrine" of Wrigley Field on the prosperous north side.

The team was a powerhouse in the early years of the AL, but it led to the worst scandal in baseball history. In 1919, eight White Sox players conspired with gamblers to lose the 1919 World Series to the Cincinnati Reds, and the group, which included the great hitter Shoeless Joe Jackson, was banned for life. The club didn't win another World Championship until 2005, although they did reach the 1959 World Series against the Los Angeles Dodgers, and won division titles in 1983, 1993, and 2000. Their last playoff appearance was in 2008.

Los Angeles Angels

Founded in 1961
Other Names: California Angels, Anaheim Angels
1 World Championship (2002)
1 AL pennant

Big spending has characterized the attempts by owner Arte Moreno to re-establish the Angels as a contender in the

AL West. His recent free-agent acquisitions include Albert Pujols, the three-time MVP with the Cardinals, and Josh Hamilton, the 2010 MVP with the Rangers, but the team has struggled to regain the form it demonstrated while making the playoffs five times between 2004 and 2009.

For the first 35 years of their existence, the Angels—who shared Los Angeles with the Dodgers before moving to Anaheim in 1966—were owned by beloved cowboy star Gene Autry. He presided over only three playoff series, excruciating losses in the AL Championship Game, before his death. The Walt Disney Company was the beneficiary of the team's surge under manager Mike Scioscia in 2002, when the Angels rallied from a 5-0 deficit in Game 6 of the World Series, and defeated the Giants in Game 7 behind rookie pitchers John Lackey, Brendan Donnelly, and Frankie Rodriguez.

Clever T-Shirt

When the Angels made their second name change in just a few years, deciding to call themselves the Los Angeles Angels of Anaheim, the Dodgers decided to have a bit of fun at the Angels' expense. They printed T-shirts that said "Los Angeles Dodgers of Los Angeles."

Famous Angel: Rod Carew, 1967–1985

HR	RBI	AVG
92	1,015	.328

Rod Carew began as a second baseman with the Twins, who converted him to first base and traded him to the Angels about halfway through his 19-year career. Though he never was much of a home run threat, Carew was known for getting on base—look at his high batting average. He even won the batting title in 1972 and is still the only AL player to win the title without hitting even one homer. Carew was appointed to the all-star team for the first 18 years that he played. He led his Angels to two LCS appearances, including their first ever in 1979. He joined the Hall of Fame in 1999, in his first year of eligibility.

Stealing Home

Rod Carew stole 353 bases in his career. Of these, 17 were steals of home—including 8 steals of home in a single season. Watch out when this guy gets to third!

Cleveland Indians

Founded in 1901
Other Names: Cleveland Blues, Bronchos, Naps
2 World Championships (1920, 1948)
5 AL pennants

Of the eight original franchises still competing in the American League, none has waited longer for a World Championship than the Indians. Not since 1948, when the owner was Bill Veeck; the manager was Lou Boudreau, a Hall of Fame shortstop; and the home park was cavernous Municipal Stadium, has the Tribe ruled over baseball. So consistently bad were the Indians during much of the 1970s and 1980s that they inspired a movie fable of unwanted castoffs called *Major League*.

However, the Indians became perennial contenders in the 1990s by signing talented young players to long-term contracts financed in part by the move to a beautiful, intimate ballpark, Jacobs Field. From 1995 through 2001, Cleveland advanced to the playoffs six times and reached the World Series in both 1995 and 1997. After a seven-game loss to the Red Sox in the 2007 ALCS, the Indians fell out of contention until 2013 when former Boston manager Terry Francona guided a largely anonymous roster to an unexpected wild card berth.

Famous Indian: Bob Feller, 1936–1956

W-L	ERA	K
266-162	3.25	2,581

Feller was the dominant American League pitcher in the years around World War II. His background as an Iowa farmer made him a strong teenager and propelled him to the majors at a young age. He struck out 17 batters in a game

FUN FACT

Sellout Streak

From 1995 until 2001, every seat at Jacobs Field was sold out every night, for 455 games in a row. Therefore, the Indians retired the number 455 in honor of their fans.

when he was only 17 years old, and he had won 20 major-league games when he was still 20 years old. Feller's career was interrupted by four years of service in the navy during the war. He returned to the field in the late 1940s and continued pitching until 1956. He claims to have thrown faster fastballs even than Nolan Ryan. Feller was sometimes unhittable, but he walked more batters than anyone else, too. He was elected to the Hall of Fame in 1962 in his first ballot.

Toronto Blue Jays

Founded in 1977
2 World Championships (1992, 1993)
2 AL pennants

Not only was it the most famous moment of club history, but it also doubles as the most famous baseball moment in the history of Canada. Although the Blue Jays were the second major-league franchise to play north of the U.S. border, following the Montreal Expos, they are the only one to win a World Series. They won two in a row and their second, in 1993, was particularly memorable. Joe Carter's three-run homer in the ninth inning of Game 6 against the Phillies was just the second time that a World Series was determined by a walk-off homer.

It marked the culmination of the Blue Jays' rise from humble beginnings as an expansion team in 1977, playing in cold Exhibition Stadium, to the modernistic SkyDome (now Rogers Centre), with its retractable roof and centerfield hotel. However, after eleven consecutive winning seasons and five trips to the playoffs, the team has struggled to succeed in the American League East, even after trading for such accomplished and highly paid players as José Reyes, Mark Buehrle, and Cy Young award winner R.A. Dickey after the 2012 season.

O, Canada!

Baseball games traditionally begin with the singing of the U.S. national anthem, "The Star-Spangled Banner." But if the Blue Jays are in town, you'll also hear the Canadian anthem "O, Canada!"

Minnesota Twins

Founded in 1901	
Other Names: Washington Senators, Washington Nationals	
3 World Championships (1924, 1987, 1991)	
6 AL pennants	

The Washington Senators were one of the AL's original eight teams. In 1961, the Senators moved to the twin cities of Minneapolis–St. Paul, Minnesota, and became the Twins. The team originally played in cold Metropolitan Stadium but moved indoors to the Metrodome in 1982.

The Metrodome helped the team win their first World Series in Minnesota. In 1987, the Twins had the best home record in the league (56-21), but on the road, they were 33-52. In the playoffs and the World Series they won every game in the Metrodome. Similarly, in 1991, the Twins beat the Braves 4-3 in the World Series, winning all four games in the Metrodome. The Twins moved to the outdoor Target Field in 2010, but the Metrodome will always hold a dear place in Twins fans' hearts.

Famous Twin: Kirby Puckett, 1984–1995

HR	RBI	AVG
207	1,085	.318

Though he was only 5'8", Kirby Puckett played baseball like a giant. His batting average was .288 in his *worst* season. He also hit for power, hitting double-digit home runs in nine of his 12 seasons. In addition to his batting skills, Puckett was known as an outstanding defensive outfielder. Highlights of his playing days show him crashing into the

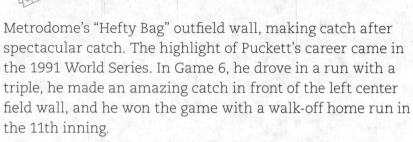

Metrodome's "Hefty Bag" outfield wall, making catch after spectacular catch. The highlight of Puckett's career came in the 1991 World Series. In Game 6, he drove in a run with a triple, he made an amazing catch in front of the left center field wall, and he won the game with a walk-off home run in the 11th inning.

In 1995, Puckett was hit in the head by a pitch, which broke his jaw. Puckett developed eye problems and never played a major-league game again. He became one of the youngest hall of famers ever when he was elected on the first ballot in 2001. Kirby Puckett died of a stroke in 2006 at age 45.

Oakland Athletics

Founded in 1901
Other Names: Philadelphia Athletics, Kansas City Athletics
9 World Championships (1910, 1911, 1913, 1929, 1930, 1972, 1973, 1974, 1989)
15 AL pennants

The Athletics, frequently shortened to A's by both fans and media, were the brainchild of one man. Connie Mack, a former catcher, served as manager, part owner, and conscience of the club during its first 50 years of existence, all in Philadelphia. He developed many great players—among them Eddie Collins, Lefty Grove, Al Simmons, and Jimmie Foxx— and fielded several great teams, earning eight pennants and five World Championships, but he couldn't afford to retain the talent.

When the A's were sold to investors from Kansas City in 1955, they were a last-place team, and stayed near the bottom of the AL throughout their 13 seasons in the Midwest. Enter Charles O. Finley, an insurance man from Indiana,

who bought the team, dressed it in gaudy gold and green uniforms, and moved it to a new stadium in Oakland. He also signed a lot of good young players. Reggie Jackson, Catfish Hunter, Joe Rudi, Sal Bando, and Rollie Fingers became the nucleus of the great A's teams that won the World Series in 1972, 1973, and 1974, the only franchise other than the Yankees to win three consecutive championships.

In the post-Finley era, the "Bash Brothers," Mark McGwire and Jose Canseco, led them to three consecutive World Series appearances, but they won only once, the 1989 Classic that was interrupted by the San Francisco Bay earthquake. In 1997, amid a dropoff in talent and falling attendance, the A's hired Billy Beane as general manager. Using an approach known as "moneyball," he resurrected the small-market team without spending a lot of money. Oakland qualified for the playoffs five times in the decade starting in 2000 and, after a few years of mediocrity, surprised baseball by winning the AL West in 2012 and 2013.

Famous Athletic: Reggie Jackson, 1967–1987

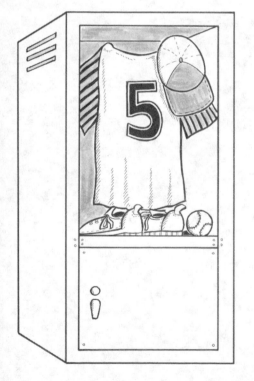

HR	RBI	AVG
563	1,702	.262

Reggie Jackson earned the nickname "Mr. October" because he was awesome when it was World Series time (in October). A great power hitter even in his rookie year in 1967, Jackson went on to lead the league in home runs four times during his career and ended up sixth on the all-time list when he retired. Jackson helped the A's win three consecutive World Series championships in 1972, 1973, and 1974. He later joined the Yankees and helped lead them to

the World Series three times and to win two more World Championships. Reggie struck out a lot and wasn't a great defensive star, but when it was an important game, he was at his best. In Game 6 of the 1977 World Series, Jackson had what many consider the single best World Series game of any hitter ever. He hit three tremendous home runs and drove in five runs in the game. Jackson was outspoken and very popular everywhere he went through his entire career. He made the Hall of Fame in 1993.

Kansas City Royals

Founded in 1969
1 World Championship (1985)
2 AL pennants

One of baseball's best franchises in the 1980s, the Royals have been searching for a winning formula ever since the deaths of manager Dick Howser in 1987, and founder/owner Ewing Kauffman in 1993. Professing the need to operate as a small-market team, they have lingered in the bottom half of the league for two decades, trading away such talented players as Carlos Beltrán, David Cone, Bret Saberhagen, Jermaine Dye, and Zack Greinke, often for financial reasons.

After three unsuccessful attempts to beat the Yankees in the AL playoffs, Whitey Herzog's team finally overcame New York to win the 1980 AL pennant, only to fall to the Phillies in the World Series. Howser, fired by the Yankees for losing the 1980 ALCS, then led the Royals back to the World Series in 1985, and defeated Herzog's Cardinals in seven games, capped by Saberhagen's shutout. A surge after the all-star break in 2013 finally lifted hopes for a brighter future.

FUN FACT

Waterfall in the Outfield

In 1973, the Royals moved into Royals Stadium, still one of the most beautiful major-league parks. It was eventually renamed for longtime owner Ewing Kauffman. There aren't very many seats in the outfield at Royals Stadium. Instead, the Water Spectacular puts on a huge waterfall show in between innings. A home run by the Royals can end up splashing!

Famous Royal: George Brett, 1973–1993

HR	RBI	AVG
317	1,595	.305

George Brett spent his entire career with the Royals, and that career coincided with the best years of the Kansas City Royals franchise. He was a .300 hitter who also hit 15–20 home runs every year. As if that weren't good enough, he was even better in the postseason. In the 1977 ALCS, he hit three home runs in the same game; he and teammate Hal McRae both rank top ten all time in World Series batting average.

Despite his awesome career, Brett might be best remembered for the pine tar incident. In 1983, he hit a go-ahead home run against the Yankees, but he was called out for using an illegal bat that had too much sticky pine tar on it. Brett charged the umpire in a crazy, spitting rage. As it turned out, the commissioner later decided that the rule about pine tar on bats wasn't clear, so the home run counted. George Brett is the only Royal in the Hall of Fame. He was inducted in 1999.

Baltimore Orioles

Founded in 1901
Other Names: Milwaukee Brewers, St. Louis Browns
3 World Championships (1966, 1970, 1983)
7 AL pennants

After a 14-year drought under six different managers, the Orioles finally posted a winning season and reached the playoffs in 2012. Buck Showalter led the franchise back to prominence with the help of a home-run surge keyed by the emergence of Chris Davis, an outstanding bullpen, and an unprecedented 29-9 record in one-run games. The relatively

young team restored the pride established by the great Baltimore clubs managed by the late Earl Weaver in the late 1960s and early 1970s.

The Orioles were mostly failures during their 52-year existence as the St. Louis Browns, qualifying for their only World Series in the war year of 1944, against the Cardinals, with whom they shared a ballpark. Unable to compete against the Cardinals for the support of the community, they moved to Baltimore in 1954. It wasn't until 1960 that the talent was sufficient to form a contender, and a trade for Frank Robinson pushed them over the top in 1966, when the slugger won a Triple Crown in batting. Robinson remained a key figure, as the Orioles won three successive pennants and a second World Series in 1970.

Famous Oriole: Cal Ripken Jr., 1981–2001

HR	RBI	AVG
431	1,695	.276

Cal Ripken Jr. was named Rookie of the Year in 1982 and MVP in 1983 and 1991. He established himself as one of the top players in modern baseball. Ripken always came to play—and play hard—day in and day out. In late 1995, he went from a star to a legend when he broke a record that most thought could never be topped. Ripken played in his 2,131st consecutive game, breaking the iron horse record set by the great Lou Gehrig. Ripken played another 501 more consecutive games before taking himself out of the lineup in September 1998.

During the 2001 season, Ripken announced his retirement after 20 years with the Orioles.

He was inducted into the Hall of Fame in 2007. In his career, Ripken played in 3,001 games and had 3,184 hits, 431 home runs, and nearly 1,700 RBIs. He was also one of the best-liked and most respected individuals who ever played in the major leagues.

Seattle Mariners

Founded in 1977
0 World Championships
0 AL pennants

Although this expansion club had a losing record in each of its first 14 years, it holds the American League standard for most victories in a regular season, 116, set in 2001. That happened to be the first year in U.S. baseball for Ichiro Suzuki, a legendary hitter from Japan, and the next-to-last in Seattle for manager Lou Piniella, who led the Mariners to their only four playoff appearances.

Under Piniella, the team enjoyed its first moment of success when the Mariners defeated the Angels in a one-game elimination for the 1995 AL West title, then rallied to defeat the Yankees in a thrilling division series. The victory, completed at the dreary Kingdome, was credited with ensuring the vote for the construction of Safeco Field, even though the Mariners subsequently lost to Cleveland in the ALCS. The club continued to win in ensuing years, despite the defections of such stars as Tino Martinez, Randy Johnson, Ken Griffey Jr., and Alex Rodriguez. None was with the team in 2001 when Ichiro, who earned both the Rookie of the Year and MVP awards, helped the team tie the record total of the 1906 Cubs. Alas, they fell short against the Yankees in the ALCS and have not returned to the playoffs.

The Mariner Moose

In 1990 the Mariners chose the Moose as their official mascot. He appears at all home games, as well as on television ads and at community events. The Mariner Moose has earned fame for his recklessness. He broke his ankle when he crashed into the outfield wall on roller skates, and he nearly ran down one of the Red Sox on his cart.

Famous Mariner: Ken Griffey Jr., 1989–2010

HR	RBI	AVG
630	1,836	.284

For a long time, people just called him "Junior," because his dad was also named Ken Griffey and was a great player for the Reds. In fact, when Griffey joined the majors in 1989, he played on the Seattle Mariners with his dad—the only time that's ever happened. Griffey, who genuinely loved to play the game, was one of the greatest center fielders ever, making many amazing catches and winning the Gold Glove for defense 10 years in a row. He was a major home run threat as well, often compared to the great Willie Mays. Griffey hit 56 home runs in 1997 and again in 1998, and he had more than 140 RBIs each year. In 2000, he joined the Cincinnati Reds, the team on which his dad became famous. Unfortunately, injury after injury slowed Junior down. Griffey hit his 500th home run in 2004, and he ended up fifth on the all-time home run list. Seattle acquired Junior from the Reds in 2009 so that he could finish his career on the team with which he is most identified.

Houston Astros

Founded in 1962
Other Names: Houston Colt .45s
0 World Championships
1 NL pennant

One year after looking up from the bottom of the National League Central division, the Astros found themselves looking up from the bottom of the American League West. One of the conditions of the team's purchase by a group

Why Astros?

In the 1960s, when the Astrodome was built, the United States was engaged in a space race, one goal of which was to send people to the moon. The control center for the U.S. space program was located in Houston. The former mayor of Houston who owned the team named the new indoor stadium the Astrodome and renamed the team the Astros. When an artificial surface was installed in the Astrodome, fake grass quickly became known as AstroTurf.

headed by Jim Crane from Drayton McLane, Jr. in 2012 was the transfer to the other league in 2013, which the Astros accomplished without a major improvement in the standings.

The Astros, originally known as the Colt .45s, joined the Mets as NL expansion teams in 1962, and took their new name after moving into baseball's first domed stadium, the Astrodome, in 1965. They didn't have any sustained success until the 1980s, when they made three playoff appearances, and lost the 1986 NLCS to their old expansion partners in an epic Game 6 settled in the 16th inning. Nineteen years later, during their sixth playoff trip in a nine-year period that featured the Killer B's—Jeff Bagwell, Craig Biggio, and Lance Berkman—the Astros defeated the Braves in 18 innings to clinch an NL division series, then lost Game 3 of their only World Series, a sweep by the White Sox, in 14 innings.

Famous Astro: Craig Biggio, 1988–2007

HR	RBI	AVG
291	1,175	.281

Craig Biggio joined the Astros in 1988 as the rare catcher who could hit well, and he made the all-star team in 1991 as a catcher. Biggio moved to second base in 1992—and made the all-star team again.

Biggio has played in more games than any other Astro. At his last game in 2007, a sold-out crowd cheered him into retirement. The Astros retired his number 7 the next year. Though he's from New York, 20 years of playing in Houston seems to have rubbed off on Biggio, who coached his sons' high school baseball teams while serving as assistant to the general manager of the Astros.

Chapter 5
Great Players of Today

One of the great things about baseball is that on any given day anyone can be the big hero. It's fun to hear about people like Bucky Dent or Francisco Cabrera, who were never stars but happened to get a hit at an incredibly important time. But the best baseball players are the hitters who get important hits every couple of nights and the pitchers who are so good so often that no one wants to hit against them. These are today's stars who could be tomorrow's Hall-of-Famers.

Premier Pitchers

Twenty years ago, a starting pitcher was expected to pitch eight or nine innings. Nowadays, relief pitchers are used a lot more, and even reliable starters often pitch only five or six innings. That hasn't changed the fact that the most important player a team can have is an "ace" starter, someone you can rely on to shut down an opponent every time he takes the mound. Here are the best of the major-league aces.

Felix Hernandez

W	ERA	K
110	3.20	1,703

A prodigy in his home country of Venezuela, Felix Hernandez was signed by the Seattle Mariners on the day he turned 16. He made his major-league debut at 19 and has been a consistent winner on a team with a losing record. His talent is so special that he was honored with the Cy Young Award as best pitcher in the American League in

WORDS to KNOW

Bugs Bunny changeup: In the famous cartoon "Baseball Bugs," Bugs Bunny enters the Polo Grounds to pitch against the Gas House Gorillas. He throws a changeup so slow that he strikes out three batters with one pitch. When a pitcher throws a changeup so slow it makes a batter look silly, it's sometimes called a "Bugs Bunny changeup."

2010, despite the fact that the Mariners' lack of run support limited him to a 13-12 record. While that team finished the season 61-101 and in last place in the AL West, Hernandez led all pitchers in games started (34), innings pitched (249.2), and earned run average (2.27 per game). His league-leading five shutouts in 2012 included a perfect game, 1-0 victory over the Rays. Nicknamed the "King" in Seattle, Hernandez pledged to remain with the struggling franchise instead of seeking an opportunity with a contending team, signing a seven-year contract extension in 2013. When he finally gets his chance to pitch in the postseason, he wants it to be in a Mariners' uniform.

Clayton Kershaw

W	ERA	K
77	2.60	1,206

It is inevitable that every lefthander to pitch for the Dodgers is measured against the great Sandy Koufax. Clayton Kershaw may be the first not to be overwhelmed by the comparison. In five of his first six seasons with the club, he posted an earned run average lower than 3. He achieved his 1,000th strikeout two months after he turned 25. A first-round draft choice out of a Texas high school in 2006, he won the Cy Young Award just five years later, when he led the National League in victories (21), strikeouts (248), and ERA (2.28). Koufax, saddled with a losing record before the age of 25, turned the number 32 into one of the most celebrated in Dodgers' history. Kershaw has the opportunity to do the same for number 22.

save: When a pitcher comes into a close ballgame and gets the final outs, that pitcher earns a save.

OPS: One statistic that baseball people have learned to focus on is OPS, which stands for "on base plus slugging." To calculate OPS, just add a player's on-base percentage to his slugging percentage. A typical OPS is about .750. The best hitters have a season-long OPS above .900, and just a few each year make it above 1.000.

WORDS to KNOW

pitching rotation: A starting pitcher can't pitch every day—his arm would get so sore it would fall off! Since games are scheduled almost every day, teams usually use a rotation of five pitchers who take turns starting.

WORDS to KNOW

Wins Above Replacement (WAR): WAR is an advanced statistic that tries to show how important a player is to his team. Although he was only a rookie in 2012, Mike Trout's WAR was 10.9, the highest number since Barry Bonds' 11.8 in 2002. That means if the Angels hadn't had Trout, the team would have had more than 10 fewer wins, and it explains why he finished second in voting for the AL MVP award to Triple Crown winner Miguel Cabrera. Even for the best players, a WAR above 7 is outstanding.

Justin Verlander

W	ERA	K
137	3.41	1,671

When Justin Verlander was selected as the Most Valuable Player in 2011, it marked the first time in 27 years that the American League gave the award to a pitcher and the first time in 40 years that it honored a starting pitcher. "All" he did the next season was lead the Detroit Tigers to a World Series appearance. The big right-hander, who starred for Old Dominion University in his native Virginia, has been the strong arm of one of the league's most successful teams. Verlander is one of only three current major-league pitchers to have tossed two no-hit games since 2007. He traditionally has been a league-leader in innings pitched and strikeouts, the very definition of an ace.

Other Starting Pitchers

As a rookie in 2006, Adam Wainwright helped St. Louis to a World Series title as a relief pitcher. Now he's among the most dependable starters on the Cardinals and a consistent All-Star. At 27, David Price has already won one Cy Young Award and is the acknowledged ace among one of baseball's best pitching staffs in Tampa Bay. Formerly the best pitcher in Japan, Yu Darvish has struck out an average of 11 batters per nine innings in two seasons with the Texas Rangers. Max Scherzer, the majors' only 20-game winner in 2013, teams with Verlander to provide the Tigers' rotation with an outstanding 1-2 punch.

Top Hitters

Miguel Cabrera

HR	RBI	AVG
365	1,260	.321

The first major-league player in 45 years to earn a Triple Crown in batting, Cabrera has become the finest overall hitter in baseball. Not since Hall of Famer Carl Yastrzemski in 1967 has a man led his league in batting average, home runs, and runs batted in. Cabrera topped all American League hitters with a .330 average, 44 homers, and 139 RBIs in 2012 while also leading the Detroit Tigers to the World Series. Signed to a professional contract at the age of 16 by the Marlins, the native of Venezuela became a rookie force in the team's surprising rise, hitting a walk-off home run in his first game and assuming the role of cleanup hitter. He has continued his development since his trade to the Tigers before the 2008 season. In Detroit, he has won consecutive batting titles and earned his first Most Valuable Player Award in 2012. Cabrera has driven in more than 100 runs in every major-league season except his first, when he played in only 87 games.

Joe Mauer

HR	RBI	AVG
105	634	.323

Mauer is the only catcher to win three batting titles in the history of major-league baseball. Not

Game Pieces

Baseball is such a familiar game that you might not even need words to describe it! Study the four picture puzzles below and see if you can figure out what baseball play, player, or place they each describe.

only is he a hometown hero, having grown up in St. Paul, Minnesota, but he also ranks among the greatest athletes in the state. He was the national player of the year in both baseball and football (he played quarterback) at Cretin-Derham Hall High School (which also produced Hall of Fame hitter Paul Molitor), where he also starred in basketball. Although a concussion suffered in August cut his season short in 2013, the former Most Valuable Player (2009) hit as efficiently as ever in 113 games before the injury. The Twins have slipped from the top of the AL Central division in recent years but not because of their star's performance.

Joey Votto

HR	RBI	AVG
157	530	.314

The Canadian-born first baseman for the Reds is the leader among active major-league players in on-base percentage. An outstanding hitter who has averaged .300 or better in all but his first full season, he has great patience at the plate and draws an average of 100 walks per year. In 2010, while leading Cincinnati to its first playoff appearance in 15 years, Votto not only won the National League's Most Valuable Player award, but was also recognized as Canada's foremost athlete. Born in Toronto, Votto also played hockey and basketball in high school, but his baseball skills were such that he was selected in the second round of baseball's 2002 amateur draft. Although he homered in his second major-league at bat in September 2007, he has become better known for doubles and hitting in the clutch.

WORDS to KNOW

MVP: MVP stands for Most Valuable Player. One player in each league wins the MVP award every year, not only for being a great player, but usually for helping their team go to the playoffs. The Baseball Writers' Association of America chooses who wins the MVP award.

Other Great Hitters

There are many other great hitters in baseball today, including a trio of youngsters—Mike Trout of the Angels, Bryce Harper of the Nationals, and Manny Machado of the Orioles—who made a major splash in 2012. Buster Posey of the Giants, who already has an MVP award, is poised to succeed Mauer as the best-hitting catcher in the sport. First baseman Chris Davis of the Orioles and Paul Goldschmidt of the Diamondbacks have developed into the game's next great sluggers. And second base, a position where offense is rarely celebrated, is bursting with offensive talent in Robinson Cano of the Yankees, Dustin Pedroia of the Red Sox, and Brandon Phillips of the Reds.

All-Time Greats Who Are Still Playing

A few players who are in the later stages of great careers are still swinging for the fences and connecting often enough to compete successfully against athletes a decade younger. Here they are, with statistics at the end of the 2013 season.

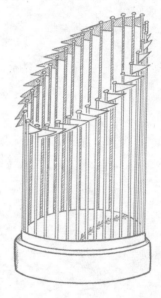

Carlos Beltran

HR	RBI	AVG
358	1,327	.283

The outfielder from Puerto Rico has been an all-star eight times with three different teams, most recently with the Cardinals at the age of 36. Beltran, the first switch-hitter in history to amass 300 home runs and 300 stolen bases, has been a terrific all-around player since winning Rookie of the

Year honors with the Royals in 1999. He has enjoyed 11 seasons with 20 or more homers, including last season, his 16th in the major leagues. A former Gold Glove centerfielder, he ranks among the best postseason hitters in history.

David Ortiz

HR	RBI	AVG
431	1,429	.287

Released by the Minnesota Twins in 2002, Ortiz developed into one of baseball's greatest sluggers with the Red Sox. In the course of 11 seasons in Boston, he has become the all-time leader in hits, home runs, and runs batted in among designated hitters. The man nicknamed Big Papi seemed to be finished when he started the 2009 season without a homer in his first 34 games, but he rebounded to hit 28 before the end of the year. An Achilles-tendon injury cost him more than a third of the 2012 season, but he starred again in 2013 at the age of 37. The Dominican native, a fan favorite in Boston and a major factor in the team's World Championships in 2004 and 2007, has hit 20 or more home runs for 12 consecutive seasons.

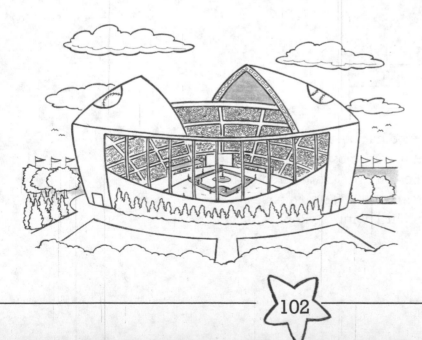

Albert Pujols

HR	RBI	AVG
492	1,498	.321

Although he has suffered through two disappointing years with the Angels and was hobbled by a foot injury in 2013, Pujols remains baseball's greatest offensive force of the 21st century. The National League Rookie of the Year in 2001, he won three Most Valuable Player awards, and led the Cardinals to two World Series titles during his 11 seasons in St. Louis. Pujols remains the only player in history to bat .300 or better, hit 30 homers, and drive in 100 runs in each of his first 10 major-league seasons. That decade of accomplishment earned him a $254 million, 10-year free agent contract from the Angels, one he has struggled to live up to in California. But at 34 and healthy again, the right-handed slugger hopes to return to form in 2014 and carry the Angels back into contention in the American League.

FUN FACT

Classic Game

For more than 40 years, Strat-O-Matic (*www.strat-o-matic.com*) has been making the ideal baseball board game. You can select your favorite team from the past season or pick up some classic teams from years gone by. There is a computerized version, but the standard version with cards and dice is still as wonderful as ever.

The Baseball Hall of Fame

In 1936, the baseball community decided that they needed a place to honor the greatest players ever. In June 1939, the National Baseball Hall of Fame and Museum was opened in Cooperstown, New York. It's a place where you'll find bats and gloves used by the greatest players, balls that were hit for historic home runs, and plenty of other neat baseball stuff. The Hall includes plaques honoring the 260 members, which include 195 major-league players along with managers and other people closely associated with the game. There are even some umpires included.

Cooperstown

How to Make It into the Hall of Fame

Making the Hall of Fame is a tremendous honor that only a small number of baseball players ever receive. A player must be retired from baseball for five years before he is eligible to be elected to the Hall. Most players are voted in by baseball writers—writers can vote for up to ten players on each year's ballot. A player who receives votes from three-fourths of the writers gets inducted into the Hall of Fame. Generally, only two or so players make the Hall of Fame each year.

There is a lot to see at the Hall, including films and even an actual ball field where two major-league teams square off every summer in a special exhibition game. The Hall of Fame also has special programs that include movies and "sandlot stories" about the game. There are also book signings by some of the many authors who write about the game, which often include former players, managers, and popular broadcasters. There's even a daily scavenger hunt for kids to take part in during the summer months. You may have to move through the Hall of Fame slowly because it's crowded, and there's so much to check out!

A Little History of the Hall

The idea for the Hall of Fame began in Cooperstown in the 1930s. Cooperstown was where Abner Doubleday, whom many credit with inventing the game, had lived, so it seemed to be the ideal place to build such a museum to honor the game. In 1936, as baseball approached its 100th anniversary, plans were made to honor the greatest players of the game. That year, five players—Ty Cobb, Babe Ruth, Honus Wagner, Christy Mathewson, and Walter Johnson—were voted in as the first players to make the Hall of Fame.

How do you get to the Baseball Hall of Fame?

To find the answer, follow the correct path from PLAY BALL to GAME OVER. Collect the letters along the way, and write them in order on the lines below.

_ _ _ _ _ _ _ ! _ _ _ _ _ _ _ ! _ _ _ _ _ _ !

FUN FACT

Baseball on TV

Baseball has figured in the plot or back-story of lots of television shows. On the old comedy *Cheers,* Sam used to be a pitcher for the Boston Red Sox. On *Seinfeld,* George worked for Yankees owner George Steinbrenner. But perhaps the most famous baseball TV show ever was the episode of *The Simpsons* in which nine major-league players decided to play for Mr. Burns's power plant softball team alongside Homer.

By 1939, the actual building was completed. There was a big ceremony that summer, and the Hall of Fame was officially opened, displaying all sorts of stuff from the game. It was a small museum at first, but thousands of people flocked to tiny Cooperstown to visit. Over the years the Hall has grown, with new wings added on to accommodate all of the new exhibits plus a gallery, a library, and more. Today, between 300,000 and 400,000 people visit the baseball shrine annually. That's quite a lot of visitors for a town whose population is only 2,300 people.

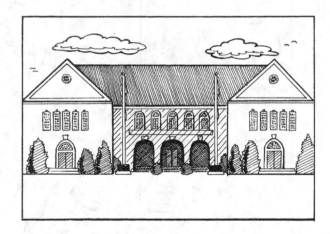

Chapter 6
The World Series

A Treasury of World Series Information

The Baseball Almanac website *www.baseball-almanac.com* includes detailed summaries of every World Series, including box scores from each game.

WORDS to KNOW

Subway Series: In New York City, most people get from place to place via the subway. When two New York teams play each other in the World Series, it's called a "Subway Series." The most recent Subway Series was in 2000, when the Yankees beat the Mets.

"The Fall Classic," as the World Series is often called, is the peak of the baseball season, when the best in the American League and the best in the National League square off for the championship of Major League Baseball. Many of baseball's greatest players have performed at their best and many of baseball's most memorable moments have occurred during the World Series. But the World Series is more than a simple means of crowning a champion. It is a national event, a yearly cultural milepost that guides the memories of many Americans.

Origins of the World Series

The World Series began in 1903, when representatives of the National League and the American League agreed to a competition that determined an overall champion. In a system that lasted through 1968, the team that won the most games in each league during the season won the pennant and the two pennant winners met in the World Series. The only playoff games required were to break ties for first place. But when the leagues expanded from 10 to 12 teams in 1969, they were divided into two divisions of six teams each. The top teams in each division participated in a playoff series, with the winners reaching the World Series. Now there are 30 major-league teams and three divisions in each league, plus three rounds of playoffs. But no matter how they get there, the survivors in each league compete in the World Series.

The Yankees have appeared in more World Series and won more championships than any other team. Between 1921 and 1964, the Yankees qualified for the World Series 29 times. Fittingly, they won the championship four times in the last five years of the 20th century, for an overall total of 27 titles.

Over a Century of the World Series

Many of baseball's most memorable moments occurred in World Series games. Here are some highlights of notable World Series events.

1903: The first World Series pitted the Pittsburgh Pirates against the Boston Americans, who were renamed the Red Sox five years later. The Americans won the series, which began on September 16, five games to three. Cy Young won two games for Boston.

1904: Manager John McGraw refused to allow his New York Giants, the NL champions, to play the AL champion Boston Americans because he said the American League was inferior. It was the first of only two years in which there was no World Series.

1905: The New York Giants defeated the Philadelphia Athletics, four games to one, with every game ending in a shutout. Giants' star Christy Mathewson threw three complete-game shutouts and walked only one batter in the most amazing pitching performance in World Series history.

1908: The Chicago Cubs beat the Detroit Tigers, four games to one, to win their second championship in as many years. They have not won a World Series since.

1918: Babe Ruth was the winning pitcher in two games as the Boston Red Sox claimed their third World Series victory in four years, beating the Chicago Cubs four games to two. The Red Sox failed to win another World Series for 86 years.

1919: The Chicago White Sox were denounced as the Black Sox after they were accused of deliberately losing the World Series to the Cincinnati Reds, five games to three, because they were paid money by gamblers. Eight White Sox players, including great hitter Joe Jackson, were banned for

Best of Seven

The World Series is played as a best-of-seven series: this means that the first team to win four games wins the Series, and there can't be more than seven games. In 1903, and again in 1919 through 1921, the Series was played as a best of nine. It returned to a best-of-seven format in 1922 and has remained so ever since.

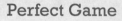

Perfect Game

A pitcher pitches a perfect game when he retires all 27 consecutive batters in a game. That's happened 21 times in the major leagues since 1900, including once in a World Series.

Lots of Games

Catcher Yogi Berra of the Yankees played 75 World Series games—more than anyone else ever has.

WORDS to KNOW

walk-off home run: When a player on the home team hits a home run in the bottom of the last inning to win the game, that player's team can walk off the field after the runs score. The game is over, regardless of how many outs are left, because the opposing team won't have a chance to score.

life from professional baseball, and the franchise didn't win another World Series until 2005.

1921: The Giants beat the Yankees, five games to three, in the first all–New York World Series. All games were played in the Polo Grounds, which served as the home field for both teams until the Yankees moved into Yankee Stadium in the Bronx two years later.

1936: The Yankees scored 18 runs in Game 2 and 13 runs in Game 6 en route to a 4-2 World Series win against their Manhattan-based rivals, the Giants. It was the Yankees' first World Series without Ruth and featured Lou Gehrig and Joe DiMaggio together for the first time in the postseason.

1944: In the final season of rosters weakened by World War II, the Cardinals defeated the Browns in the first and only all–St. Louis World Series, four games to two. All games were played at Sportsman's Park, the home field of both teams until the Browns moved to Baltimore in 1954.

1954: In the first game of the Series between the New York Giants and the Cleveland Indians, Willie Mays made what many consider baseball's most famous catch, running to the deepest part of center field at the Polo Grounds and snaring a Vic Wertz drive with his back to home plate to keep the score tied. The Giants went on to win that game and the next three over the favored Indians for a four-game sweep.

1955: After losing to the Yankees in their previous five World Series appearances, the Dodgers finally won their only championship in Brooklyn. Duke Snider hit four homers, and Johnny Podres pitched two complete-game victories, including a Game 7 shutout at Yankee Stadium.

1956: Journeyman Don Larsen of the Yankees pitched the only perfect game in World Series history in Game 5 and his team defeated the Brooklyn Dodgers one last time in seven games. The Dodgers moved to Los Angeles after the 1957 season.

The "Whole World" Series

While the World Series is played here in America, baseball is popular all over the world! See if you can match the country names with their location to fill in the grid. We left you the W-O-R-L-D S-E-R-I-E-S to help.

TOGO   MEXICO
PERU   ITALY
EGYPT   TAIWAN
IRAN   CANADA
COOK ISLANDS
PUERTO RICO
RUSSIA

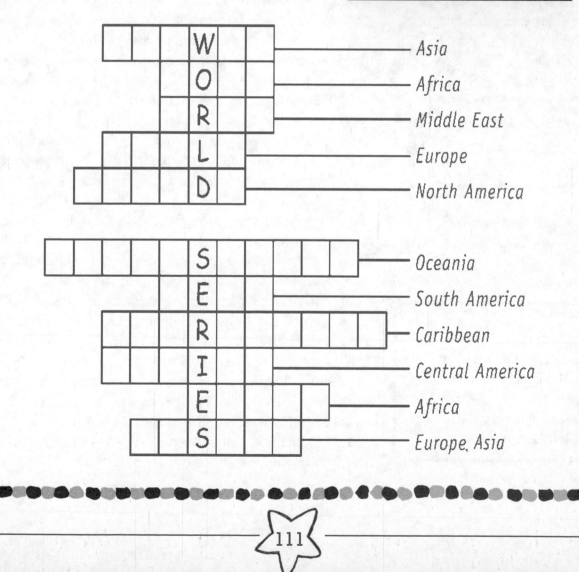

- Asia
- Africa
- Middle East
- Europe
- North America

- Oceania
- South America
- Caribbean
- Central America
- Africa
- Europe, Asia

FUN FACT

Bucky Dent

The Yankees and the Red Sox ended the 1978 season tied for first place in the American League East. They played one game to decide which team went to the playoffs. The Yankees shortstop, Bucky Dent, hit only five home runs all season. But he hit the biggest homer of his career to win the game for the Yankees and extend the Curse of the Bambino.

Seven Wins

Cardinals pitcher Bob Gibson won seven World Series games, even though his team made only three trips to the Series. In one game he struck out 17 batters.

1960: Second baseman Bill Mazeroski hit the first World Series–winning walk-off home run in history in the ninth inning of Game 7, lifting the Pirates to a championship over the mighty Yankees despite being outscored 55-27.

1966: An amazing Baltimore Orioles pitching staff shut out the Los Angeles Dodgers in the final three games of a four-game sweep. The Dodgers scored only two runs and collected a total of 17 hits, batting an anemic .142.

1969: Known as the worst team in baseball over the first seven years of their existence, the New York Mets stunned the baseball world by winning 100 games in the regular season, then beating the favored Orioles, four games to one. Game 3 featured two amazing catches by Mets center fielder Tommie Agee.

1975: It's a classic instance of baseball drama, one that has been replayed on television year after year: Carlton Fisk attempted to wave his drive fair. The Hall of Fame catcher staved off elimination for the Red Sox in Game 6 with a 12th-inning homer over Fenway Park's Green Monster. However, after falling behind early, the Cincinnati Reds rallied in Game 7 to win a thrilling World Series in which one run decided five games.

1977: Reggie Jackson, a member of three championship teams with the Oakland A's earlier in the decade, hit three consecutive home runs for the Yankees in a deciding Game 6 against the Los Angeles Dodgers. The slugger hit five homers and batted .450 in the Series, adding to his reputation as "Mr. October."

1980: Relief ace Tug McGraw struck out batters with the bases loaded in Games 5 and 6, nailing down the Phillies' first World Championship. Future Hall of Famers Steve Carlton and Mike Schmidt starred in Philadelphia's victory over the Kansas City Royals, four games to two.

1986: Down to their final out in the 10th inning of Game 6, the Mets completed a remarkable three-run comeback to beat the Red Sox, when Mookie Wilson hit a ground ball through first baseman Bill Buckner's legs, scoring Ray Knight to force a seventh game. The Mets also overcame a 3-0 deficit to win Game 7 and the World Series.

1988: A gimpy Kirk Gibson pinch-hit a two-run, walk-off homer against Hall of Fame relief ace Dennis Eckersley to win Game 1 for the Dodgers, who rolled to a stunning World Series victory in five games over the favored Oakland A's.

1989: What made the first San Francisco Bay Series so memorable was the powerful earthquake that struck less than an hour before the start of Game 3 at Candlestick Park. The Series was postponed for 10 days while a massive cleanup ensued on both sides of the Bay. When it resumed, the Oakland A's made quick work of the Giants, completing a four-game sweep.

1993: For only the second time in history, the World Series ended on a walk-off home run. It came off the bat of Toronto slugger Joe Carter and provided the Blue Jays with an 8-6 victory over the Phillies in the sixth and deciding game and their second consecutive championship.

1995: In the first World Series after the 1994 Fall Classic was canceled because of a players' strike, the Braves earned their initial championship since moving to Atlanta in 1966. Although they won a record 14 consecutive division titles, and advanced to the World Series five times between 1991 and 2005, they won the Series only once, defeating the Cleveland Indians in six games, as Tom Glavine and Mark Wohlers combined on a one-hit, 1-0 shutout.

2000: Derek Jeter homered twice and batted .409 as the Yankees dismissed the Mets in five games in the first New York "Subway Series" since 1956. Luis Sojo's two-run single in the ninth inning of Game 5 snapped a 2-2 tie and provided

The Closer

Yankee relief pitcher John Wetteland became the first pitcher ever to save all four wins for his team in the 1996 World Series against Atlanta.

FUN FACT

Marathon Match-Ups

Games 3 and 4 of the 2004 ALCS were two of the longest playoff games in history. The Yankees and the Red Sox played almost 11 hours of baseball in two days! But neither game holds the record for longest playoff game. In 2005, the Astros beat the Braves after an exhilarating 18-inning game that ran for 5 hours and 50 minutes.

the Yankees with their fourth championship in five years and 26th overall.

2001: The attacks on the World Trade Center and the Pentagon interrupted the final month of the season, pushing the World Series between the Yankees and the Arizona Diamondbacks into November for the first time. Game 3, the first Fall Classic game in New York since the horrific events of 9/11, was of such symbolic importance that President George W. Bush threw out the ceremonial first pitch from the Yankee Stadium mound. Down 2-0, the Yankees won all three home games with the help of two-out, two-run ninth-inning homers on consecutive nights by Tino Martinez and Scott Brosius. Behind the stalwart pitching of Randy Johnson and Curt Schilling, the Diamondbacks clinched the championship in only their fourth year of existence by winning the final two games in Arizona, including a ninth-inning Game 7 comeback against the great closer, Mariano Rivera, capped by a Luis Gonzalez bloop single (a weakly hit fly ball that drops in for a single between an infielder and an outfielder).

2002: Fresh off a 46-homer regular season and one year after setting the all-time record of 73, Barry Bonds capped his first successful postseason by batting .471 in the World Series with four home runs and 13 walks. He appeared on the verge of delivering the Giants' first championship to the Giants since they moved to San Francisco when the team took a 5-0 lead over Anaheim into the seventh inning Game 6. But the Angels rallied for three runs in both the seventh and eighth innings to tie the Series at three wins apiece and then coasted to a 4-1 victory in Game 7.

2004: On the brink of being swept by the Yankees in the ALCS, the Boston Red Sox rallied in the ninth inning of Game 4, and became the first team in baseball history to win a best-of-seven series after losing the first three games.

Name Change

In 1919, the Chicago White Sox were accused of being paid to lose the World Series! After that, the team became known by another name. Fill in all the letters that are not W-H-I-T-E to find out what it was.

BWLHAICTKESOX

They carried the momentum into and through the World Series, never trailing for an inning while sweeping the St. Louis Cardinals behind the hitting of Manny Ramirez (.412). The first championship for the Sox since 1918 was said to exorcise the so-called Curse of the Bambino.

2009: In the first World Series played at the new Yankee Stadium, erected across the street from the historic baseball palace, the home team defeated the Phillies, four games to two, thanks largely to Hideki Matsui. Although the popular slugger from Japan batted a remarkable .615 with three home runs to lead the Yankees to their 27th championship, the franchise declined to re-sign him.

FUN FACT

Hard Luck Teams

Through most of your lifetime, even through your parents and grandparents' lifetimes, major-league baseball has told the story of three hard-luck teams: the Red Sox, the White Sox, and the Cubs. These teams had been good back in the 1900s and 1910s, but hadn't won a championship since then. All of a sudden, though, luck seems to have changed: the Red Sox won in 2004 and 2007; the White Sox won in 2005. Could the Cubs be next?

2010: Thirteen years after driving in the World Series–winning run for the Marlins in 1997, shortstop Edgar Rentería batted .412 and was honored as the MVP of the Giants' first championship in San Francisco. The Giants' outstanding pitching staff, led by Cy Young winner Tim Lincecum and relief ace Brian Wilson, limited the hard-hitting Rangers to one run and six hits over the final two games of the five-game series.

2011: Although the Cardinals didn't qualify for the playoffs until the final day of the season, they earned their 11th World Series title, the most by a National League club. Facing elimination in Game 6, they tied the Texas Rangers on David Freese's triple with two outs in the ninth inning. Down to the final strike once more in the 10th inning, they tied the score on Lance Berkman's single. Freese then homered in the 11th to knot the Series at three wins apiece, and the Cardinals won Game 7, 6-2, in Tony La Russa's final game as a manager.

2012: After rallying from a 2-0 deficit in the NLDS and a 3-1 deficit in the NLCS, the Giants led from the start in the World Series. Third baseman Pablo Sandoval, who was benched in the 2010 Series, hit three homers in Game 1, including two off Detroit ace Justin Verlander, and the Giants swept the Tigers. Madison Bumgarner and Ryan Vogelsong started consecutive shutouts in Games 2 and 3; and Marco Scutaro, a midseason pickup, singled across the winning run in the 10th inning of Game 4.

2013: One year after finishing last in their division, the Boston Red Sox completed a remarkable turnaround with a World Series victory over the St. Louis Cardinals in six games. MVP David Ortiz dominated the offense with 11 hits and eight walks in 25 plate appearances for a stunning .760 on-base percentage and starting pitcher Jon Lester allowed only one run in his two victories. It marked the team's third World Championship in 10 years, but the first clinched in historic Fenway Park since 1918, when Babe Ruth was the pitching star.

Chapter 7
Statistics and Records

More than any other sport, statistics are very much a part of baseball. Since the beginning of the sport, fans have wanted to know who had the most hits, who made the error, who got the win, and so on. Home run totals, batting averages, wins, strikeouts—they are all a central part of baseball's popularity. Sometimes when a player was on the verge of breaking a record, like when Cal Ripken Jr. played in his 2,131st game, or when Hank Aaron hit home run number 715, or even when Derek Jeter got his 3,000th hit, the individual achievements of the players got more attention than the ballgame. That's part of what makes baseball so interesting. Your team may not be doing well, like the Giants in 2006, but you might want to watch them anyway to see a slugger like Barry Bonds pile up home runs on his way to a record.

There's a stat for everything in baseball. You could probably find the answer to "What pitcher threw the most wild pitches in night games at Wrigley Field in the 1940s?" Okay, so that's a trick question—there were no night games at Wrigley in the 1940s because they had no lights. But the point is that if you love statistics you could probably spend a year looking at baseball statistics and never see the same one twice.

Individual Stats

Players' individual statistics, or "stats," are followed closely, not only by fans but also by sportswriters, team management, and everyone associated with baseball. There are actually thousands of statistics that are recorded, from how long it took to play a game to how many times a hitter grounded out to the shortstop. Many baseball stats, such

FUN FACT

Back-to-Back No-Hitters!

The only pitcher ever to throw no-hitters in two starts in a row was Johnny Vander Meer of the Cincinnati Reds in 1938.

as batting average or runs batted in, have been kept and published since the late 19th and early 20th centuries. Others, like saves and holds, have been devised in more recent years. Computers have made it easy to quickly calculate somewhat more obscure statistics, such as slugging percentage or batting average with runners in scoring position. The following are the most common player statistics you will see in the sports pages. Statistics for each game are usually found in what was termed back in the 1800s as a "box score," or a summary of the game in a box. More than 100 years later, whether you find box scores in the newspaper or online, they are still the most popular way to see what happened in a ballgame.

> ### STATS, LLC
>
> STATS, LLC is a company that maintains baseball statistics. They have reporters at every game who record the result of every pitch. Each year they publish several books filled with stats and scouting reports of current players.

Box Score

On Monday, November 1, 2010, the San Francisco Giants and Texas Rangers played Game 5 of the World Series at Rangers Ballpark in Arlington, Texas. Going into the game, the Giants led the series 3-1, so the Giants knew if they won the game, they would be World Champions. Super pitchers Cliff Lee and Tim Lincecum both pitched scoreless games through six innings. In the seventh, Giants shortstop Edgar Rentería hit a three-run shot with two out, leading to a Giants championship.

Across the top is the inning-by-inning account of runs scored. You'll see that the Giants got 3 in the top of the seventh, but the Rangers could only get 1 in the bottom of the seventh.

Box Scores

Team	1 2 3	4 5 6	7 8 9	R H E
San Francisco Giants	0 0 0	0 0 0	3 0 0	3 7 0
Texas Rangers	0 0 0	0 0 0	1 0 0	1 3 1

Giants

NAME	ab	r	h	rbi
Torres rf	4	0	1	0
Sanchez 2b	4	0	1	0
Posey c	4	0	2	0
Ross lf	4	1	1	0
Uribe 3b	4	1	1	0
Huff 1b	3	0	0	0
Burrell dh	4	0	0	0
Rentería ss	3	1	1	3
Rowand cf	3	0	0	0
Total	33	3	7	3

Rangers

NAME	ab	r	h	rbi
Andrus ss	4	0	0	0
Young 3b	4	0	1	0
Hamilton cf	4	0	0	0
Guerrero dh	4	0	0	0
Cruz rf	4	1	1	1
Kinsler 2b	2	0	0	0
Murphy lf	3	0	0	0
Molina c	3	0	0	0
Moreland 1b	2	0	1	0
Total	30	1	3	1

E – Moreland. GIDP – Rentería. LOB – San Francisco 4, Texas 4. HR – Rentería, Cruz. SAC – Huff.

PITCHERS

Giants

NAME	ip	h	r	er	bb	so
Lincecum (W, 4-1)	8	3	1	1	2	10
Wilson (S, 6)	1	0	0	0	0	2

Rangers

NAME	ip	h	r	er	bb	so
Lee (L, 3-2)	7	6	3	3	0	6
Feliz	2	1	0	0	0	2

Umpires: HP – Kellogg, 1b – Darling, 2b – Hirschbeck, 3b – Holbrook, lf – Miller, rf – Winters. Time of game – 2:32. Attendance: 52,045.

R, H, and E are runs, hits, and errors for each team for the game.

The rest of the abbreviations are as follows:

Pos is the position that player played. If you see two people at the same position, that means the second player is a substitute.

You may wonder what this all means. Well, it's very simple once you learn about the format.

Across the top is the inning-by-inning account of runs scored.

The positions are:

1b	First base
2b	Second base
3b	Third base
ss	Shortstop
lf	Left fielder
cf	Center fielder
rf	Right fielder
c	Catcher
p	Pitcher
ph	Pinch hitter (someone who bats for another player)
pr	Pinch runner (someone who runs for someone else)
dh	The American League and some minor leagues use designated hitters, who bat for the pitchers. Since this game was played at an American League team's field, the DH was used.

The rest of the stats tell you what each player did in the game.

ab	At bats, or how many times the batter officially had a turn at bat (walks, sacrifices, and being hit by a pitch don't count as official at bats)
r	Runs scored
h	Hits

The Ultimate Inning

In 1999, Fernando Tatis of the St. Louis Cardinals hit a grand slam home run. His team kept on hitting and scoring runs in the inning, so he got to bat again in the same inning with the bases loaded. Believe it or not, he hit another grand slam, becoming the first player ever to hit two grand slam home runs and drive in eight runs in one inning. Wow!

batting average: A player's batting average, sometimes listed in the box score, is a good measure of his ability to hit. The best hitters have a .300 average or better, while a player hitting .200 might be sent back to the minor leagues. No one has hit .400 for an entire season since Ted Williams hit .406 in 1941. To calculate a batting average, divide a player's hits by his at bats.

I'll Play Anywhere

Only two players in baseball history have played all ten positions. That's right, ten ... Bert Campaneris of the A's and Cesar Tovar of the Twins not only played all nine defensive positions, including one pitching appearance each, but they were also designated hitters.

rbi	Runs batted in (a hit or another play that brings in runs)
bb	Base on balls (or walks)
so	Strikeouts, also sometimes listed as "k"
avg	Batting average

There will also be some information listed underneath the line that says "totals," telling you who hit doubles (2B), triples (3B), and home runs (HR) and how many of each the player has for the season or the playoffs. You'll also see if a player had a sacrifice (SAC) or a sacrifice fly (SF), or if he grounded into a double play (GIDP). Players don't like to see it, but there is also a listing of errors (E) as well. Stolen bases (SB), caught stealing (CS), and runners the team left on base (LOB) are listed next. Many box scores may give you more detailed information, but these are the basics.

Pitching statistics are included toward the bottom. You'll often find next to pitchers' names the "decision," meaning the win (W) or loss (L), or the save (S) for a reliever. In the game previously described, Lincecum was the winning pitcher and Wilson earned the save. Lee was the losing pitcher. His win-loss record is listed as 3-2, or three wins and two losses for the playoffs.

Other numbers you may see next to the name are:

| bs | Blown saves, which tell you how many times the pitcher has failed to save a game. |
| h | Hold, an unofficial statistic, will show up for relief pitchers. It means they held the lead until the closer came in and finished the game. |

Then you'll see what is called the "pitcher's line" for the game, which includes:

sacrifice: When a batter bunts, allowing himself to be thrown out but advancing runners, he is credited with a sacrifice. A sacrifice does not count as a time at bat.

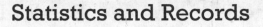 

ip	Innings pitched. Sometimes you'll see a decimal like 7.1, meaning the pitcher lasted seven innings and got one out in the eighth. 7.2 would mean he got two outs in the eighth.
h	Hits allowed
r	Runs allowed
er	Earned runs allowed. Not all runs count as "earned runs." If an error on a play put a future scorer on base or helped a runner to score, that run does not count toward a pitcher's ERA. In the game mentioned earlier, the errors didn't allow any runs to score, so all runs were earned.
bb	Base on balls, or walks allowed
so	Strikeouts (sometimes listed as "k")
era	The up-to-date earned run average of the pitcher, or how many earned runs he allows per nine innings. Pitchers try to keep their ERAs under 4.00, which is getting harder to do. Starting pitchers pitch more innings, so it's harder for them to keep those ERAs down. An ERA under 3.50 is quite good, especially for a starting pitcher, and under 3.00 is excellent.

Now check out the newspaper or your favorite online sports site to find more box scores. Even if you didn't watch or listen to the game, you can figure out what happened or what your favorite player did. Reading box scores is the best way to keep up with what's happening in major-league baseball.

Player Statistics

If you look up a player on the Internet or in a baseball book (including this one), you'll find ballplayers' statistics for each season and for their careers.

WORDS to KNOW

ERA: ERA stands for a pitcher's earned run average, or how many runs that pitcher is likely to give up in a full nine-inning game. To calculate ERA, multiply the number of earned runs allowed by 9; then divide by the number of innings pitched.

assist: When a player makes a throw of any kind to get an out, whether it's an infielder throwing a batter out at first base or an outfielder throwing out a runner at home plate, the fielder gets credit for an assist.

putout: The fielder who catches a fly ball, steps on the base, or applies a tag to actually put the runner out gets credit for a putout.

FUN FACT

Shutouts

A pitcher earns a shutout by holding the opposing team without a run for the whole game. The pitcher who threw the most shutouts in baseball history was Walter Johnson, "the Big Train," who blanked the other team 110 times in his career.

WORDS to KNOW

fielding percentage: One measure of a fielder's strength is the fielding percentage. To calculate this stat, add the player's putouts and assists. Then, divide by the total of the player's putouts, assists, and errors. A good fielder will have a fielding percentage of .980 or .990. Outfielders are expected to have higher fielding percentages than infielders.

The most commonly found stats for hitters include everything in the box score and:

G   Games played

AVG   Batting average

SB   Stolen bases

You might also see SLG, or slugging percentage, which takes one point for each single, two for each double, three for each triple, and four for each home run, adds them up and divides by the number of at bats. Unlike batting averages, which rarely top .350, slugging percentages for the best power hitters can reach .600 or higher.

Common pitching stats include everything in the box score and:

G   Games pitched in

GS   Games started

CG   Complete games

Sho   Shutouts (held the opposing team to no runs)

The same statistics listed for a player can also be found for a team. The stats listed here are the basics, but you can find more in books that go into greater detail.

The Standings

To follow your favorite team, you can look in the newspaper at the sports pages or on a website like Baseball Reference (*www.baseball-reference.com*) to get plenty of information including the standings—this means a list of the teams in first place through last place.

The major leagues today are each broken into three divisions:

American League

East	Central	West
Baltimore Orioles	Chicago White Sox	Los Angeles Angels
Boston Red Sox	Cleveland Indians	Oakland Athletics
New York Yankees	Detroit Tigers	Seattle Mariners
Tampa Bay Rays	Kansas City Royals	Texas Rangers
Toronto Blue Jays	Minnesota Twins	Houston Astros

National League

East	Central	West
Atlanta Braves	Chicago Cubs	Arizona Diamondbacks
Miami Marlins	Cincinnati Reds	Colorado Rockies
Washington Nationals	Milwaukee Brewers	Los Angeles Dodgers
New York Mets	Pittsburgh Pirates	San Diego Padres
Philadelphia Phillies	St. Louis Cardinals	San Francisco Giants

Other Columns You May See in the Standings Chart

- **Division:** the team's record against teams in their own division
- **Home/Road:** the team's record when playing at their home park, and the team's record when playing away from home
- **Interleague:** the team's record in games against the other league
- **Streak:** how many games the team has won or lost in a row
- **Last 10:** the team's record in their last 10 games

When you look at the standings in the papers, you'll see how many wins and losses the team has and their winning percentage, meaning what percentage of all the games they've played that they've won.

Lucky Numbers

Baseball is a game full of numbers. There's the RBI and ERA numbers, the numbers on the scoreboard, and of course the lucky number on the shirt of your favorite player!

In this tricky little puzzle, you must figure out what lucky combination of numbers to use so that each column (up and down) or row (across) adds up to the right totals shown in the white numbers. The white arrows show you in which direction you will be adding. Lucky you—four numbers are in place to get you started!

Here are the rules:

- You are only adding the numbers in any set of white boxes that are touching each other.
- Use only the numbers 1 through 9. Each number can only be used *once* in each set.
- Remember that each answer has to be correct both across *and* down!

9↓ 24↓   27↓ 13↓

12→

5→

11→   6   15→ 9

            6↓

17→

15↓

16→ 7   12→   11↓ 8

13→   4→

Games Behind

When you look at the standings, you will also see the abbreviation "GB" (games behind), which is a way of judging how close your team is to first place in their division. Games behind means how many times your team would have to beat the first place team in order to catch up with them. You might see:

Team	W-L	GB
New York Yankees	60-40	——
Boston Red Sox	58-42	2
Baltimore Orioles	54-48	7
Toronto Blue Jays	49-50	?
Tampa Bay Rays	40-60	?

How do you figure this out?

You subtract how many games the teams are apart in wins and then do the same for losses. In the first example, you can figure out the difference between the Yankees and Red Sox.

In wins you have 60 – 58 = 2.

In losses you have 42 – 40 = 2.

Then add the two numbers you came up with together: 2 + 2 = 4.

Then divide by 2: 4 ÷ 2 = 2.

The Red Sox are therefore 2 games behind the Yankees.

That one was easy because they were 2 games apart in wins and in losses. Sometimes teams will have played different numbers of games at a certain time in the season because of their schedules and because sometimes games are rained out.

WORDS to KNOW

sacrifice fly: When a batter hits a fly ball deep enough to allow a runner on third to tag up and score, he is credited with a sacrifice fly. A sacrifice fly does not count as a time at bat.

To see how many games back the Orioles are behind the Yankees, you would use the same formula.

Wins, 60 – 54 = 6.
Losses, 48 – 40 = 8.
Then add them together: 6 + 8 = 14.
Then divide by 2: 14 ÷ 2 = 7.
The Orioles are 7 games behind the Yankees.

Now, without looking below, try to figure out how far the Blue Jays are behind the Yankees.

Wins, 60 – 49 = 11.
Losses, 50 – 40 = 10.
11 + 10 = 21.
21 ÷ 2 = 10.5

Now you try Tampa Bay! (In case you're wondering, Tampa Bay is 20 games out.)

Secret Signals

Use the decoder to figure out what message the catcher signaled to the pitcher when the crab came up to bat.

A G N S
C H O T
E I P U
F L R Y

All-Time Record Holders

These records are correct as of the start of the 2014 season.

Hitting

All-Time Batting Average Leaders
1. Ty Cobb .366
2. Rogers Hornsby .358
3. Shoeless Joe Jackson .356
4. Lefty O'Doul .349
5. Ed Delahanty .346
6. Tris Speaker .345
7. Ted Williams .344
8. Billy Hamilton .344
9. Dan Brouthers .342
10. Babe Ruth .342

A player must have more than 3,000 plate appearances to qualify for this list.

All-Time RBI Leaders
1. Hank Aaron 2,297
2. Babe Ruth 2,213
3. Cap Anson 2,076
4. Barry Bonds 1,996
5. Lou Gehrig 1,995
6. Alex Rodriguez 1,969
7. Stan Musial 1,951
8. Ty Cobb 1,938
9. Jimmie Foxx 1,922
10. Eddie Murray 1,917

All-Time Home Run Leaders
1. Barry Bonds 762
2. Hank Aaron 755
3. Babe Ruth 714
4. Willie Mays 660
5. Alex Rodriguez 654
6. Ken Griffey Jr. 630
7. Jim Thome 612
8. Sammy Sosa 609
9. Frank Robinson 586
10. Mark McGwire 583

Best Live-Ball ERA?

Most of the ERA leaders are from the "Dead-Ball Era," when the ball was softer and harder to hit with power. This era lasted until about 1920. So who of the more recent pitchers ranks best in ERA? Mariano Rivera, who comes in 13th of all time.

WAR (Position Players)

1. Babe Ruth 183.8
2. Barry Bonds 162.5
3. Willie Mays 156.1
4. Ty Cobb 151.2
5. Hank Aaron 142.4
6. Tris Speaker 133.9
7. Honus Wagner 130.6
8. Stan Musial 128.1
9. Rogers Hornsby 127.0
10. Eddie Collins 124.0

Most Hits: Pete Rose at 4,256, followed by Ty Cobb at 4,191. They are the only two players with more than 4,000 hits!

Most Grand Slam Home Runs: Alex Rodriguez 24

Most Stolen Bases: Rickey Henderson 1,406

Most At Bats: Pete Rose 14,053

Most Seasons Played: Nolan Ryan 27

Pitching

All-Time Wins Leaders	All-Time Strikeout Leaders
1. Cy Young 511	1. Nolan Ryan 5,714
2. Walter Johnson 417	2. Randy Johnson 4,875
T3. Grover Alexander 373	3. Roger Clemens 4,672
T3. Christy Mathewson 373	4. Steve Carlton 4,136
5. Pud Galvin 365	5. Bert Blyleven 3,701
6. Warren Spahn 363	6. Tom Seaver 3,640
7. Kid Nichols 361	7. Don Sutton 3,574
8. Greg Maddux 355	8. Gaylord Perry 3,534
9. Roger Clemens 354	9. Walter Johnson 3,508
10. Tim Keefe 342	10. Greg Maddux 3,371

FUN FACT

Consecutive Scoreless Innings

Dodgers pitcher Orel Hershiser threw 59 straight innings without giving up a run in September of 1988, breaking Dodger Don Drysdale's previous record.

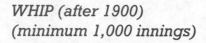 
WHIP (after 1900)
(minimum 1,000 innings)

1. Addie Joss 0.9678
2. Ed Walsh 0.9996
3. Mario Rivera 1.0003
4. Pedro Martinez 1.0544
5. Christy Mathewson 1.0581
6. Trevor Hoffman 1.0584
7. Walter Johnson 1.0612
8. Mordecai Brown 1.0658
9. Reb Russell 1.0800
10. Smoky Joe Wood 1.0869

WAR (Pitchers)

1. Cy Young 170.3
2. Walter Johnson 152.3
3. Roger Clemens 139.4
4. Grover Alexander 117
5. Kid Nichols 116.6
6. Lefty Grove 109.9
7. Tom Seaver 106.3
8. Greg Maddux 104.6
9. Randy Johnson 104.3
10. Phil Niekro 97.4

Lowest All-Time ERA: (2,000 or more innings) Ed Walsh 1.82
Most All-Time Saves: Mariano Rivera at 643 (Saves became an official statistic in 1969.)
Most No-Hitters: Nolan Ryan 7

One-Season Records

Hitting

Most Doubles: Earl Webb 67, Boston Red Sox 1931
Most Triples: Chief Wilson 36, Pittsburgh Pirates 1912
Most Home Runs: Barry Bonds 73, San Francisco Giants 2001
Most Runs Batted In: Hack Wilson 191, Chicago Cubs 1930
Most Hits: Ichiro Suzuki 262, Seattle Mariners 2004
Highest Batting Average (500+ Plate Appearances): Hugh Duffy .438, 1894

Manager Wins

The manager with the most all-time wins is Connie Mack, who won 3,731 games over 53 years between 1894 and 1950. His record has a lot to do with the many years he was a manager—he actually lost more games than he won! On the other hand, Joe McCarthy managed teams to 2,125 wins, but he only lost 1,333 games for a winning percentage of .615—the best of all time.

Highest Average (500+ Plate Appearances) since 1900:
Rogers Hornsby .424, St. Louis Cardinals 1924

Most Stolen Bases: Rickey Henderson 130, Oakland Athletics 1982

Pitching (After 1900)

Most Wins: Jack Chesbro 41, New York Highlanders 1904

Most Strikeouts: Nolan Ryan 383, California Angels 1973; Sandy Koufax 382, Los Angeles Dodgers, 1965

Lowest Earned Run Average: Dutch Leonard .96, Boston Red Sox 1914

Most Shutouts: Grover Alexander 16, Philadelphia Phillies 1916

Most Saves: Francisco Rodriguez 62, Los Angeles Angels 2008

Lowest WHIP: Pedro Martinez 0.7373, Boston Red Sox 2000

Highest WAR: Walter Johnson 16.0, Washington Senators 1913

How come Drew never finishes a baseball game?

To find out, cross out all the words that have three letters or the letter U!

AND	EVERY	CAT
TIME	GOT	HE
BAT	GETS	FAR
TO	FUR	THIRD
BUT	BASE	HIT
HE	HAT	GOES
HUT	HOME	BAG

Chapter 8
Keeping Score

Keeping score is a fun way to keep track of what's happening on the field, and it will give you a lasting record of the game you watched. You can buy scorecards at the ballpark, or make your own on a sheet of graph paper. To make life a little easier, you can use the one in this book as a model. The most important thing is that you have a place to write the name of each player and boxes for all nine (or more) innings so that you can put down what they do with each at bat. Names run down the left side of the page and innings run across the top. Why not try scoring the next game you go to?

Scoring Symbols

Scoring is pretty easy once you know the symbols to put in the boxes. You are writing down what the batter does each time he bats. Most of the time you will be listing hits or outs. When the batter makes an out, he either hit the ball to a fielder, or he struck out. For scoring purposes, the fielders are numbered—this number has nothing to do with the numbers the players are wearing on their uniforms; instead, it describes the position played by each player:

Numbers for fielding
1. Pitcher
2. Catcher
3. First baseman
4. Second baseman
5. Third baseman
6. Shortstop
7. Left fielder
8. Center fielder
9. Right fielder

Scorebooks

A scorebook is a book full of scorecards. Some people keep score of their favorite team's games in the same book all year. Some families take a scorebook to all the games they attend, then ask players to autograph the pages. You can buy scorebooks at sporting goods stores.

WORDS to KNOW

pickoff: If the pitcher throws to a base and gets the runner out before he can get back to the base, it's called a pickoff. To score a pickoff at first base, write PO 1-3, meaning pickoff, pitcher to first baseman.

Let's say the ball is hit in the air to the center fielder and he makes the catch for an out. You would put "8" in the box on your scorecard. If the ball went to right field, you'd put "9," and if it went to left field, you'd put "7." If the player pops it up and it's caught by the first baseman, you'd put "3." If the second baseman catches it, you'd put "4." A line drive to the first baseman could be scored "3L."

If the ball is hit on the ground to the shortstop and he throws to first, you put down both numbers since they were both part of the play. Therefore, a groundout to shortstop would be "6-3." A groundout to second base would be "4-3." A groundout to third base is "5-3." If the first baseman picked up a groundball and the pitcher came over to cover first base, caught the throw, and stepped on the base for the out, it would be scored "3-1," because the first baseman is "3" and the pitcher is "1." A double play that goes from the shortstop to the second baseman to the first baseman would be scored "DP 6-4-3."

Whatever fielders are involved in making the out are included in your scoring. Once you know the fielders' numbers it becomes very easy.

Hits can be scored in a few ways. A single is either "1B" or a single line (–), a double is "2B" or a double line (=), a triple is 3B or a triple line (≡), and a home run is "HR" or four lines (≣)

When runners get on base you keep track of them using the diamond in the box on the scorecard.

Just draw a line for each base they get to. For example, if a player reaches first base, you would draw the line going from home to first base. If he moves to second base when the next hitter gets a single, you would darken the line going from first base to second base.

As the players move around the bases, you draw the lines of the diamond to follow them. For every run scored you make a complete diamond. If a player is tagged out or stranded on base at the end of the inning, you just leave the diamond incomplete.

There are many, many variations on scoring. Sportswriters, broadcasters, fans, and official team statisticians are all keeping score, and they're all doing it in a slightly different manner from each other. Since there are so many ways to score, there are hundreds of different styles of scorecards. As long as you can follow what is going on in the game and you are having fun, that's all that really matters.

WORDS to KNOW

intentional walk: Sometimes the pitcher walks a batter on purpose; this is called an intentional walk. Sometimes an intentional walk makes it easier to get a double play; other times, the pitcher walks a good hitter so he can pitch to a weaker hitter later in the lineup. Score an intentional walk as "IW" or "IBB."

How to Score Hits

On the sample scorecard later in the chapter, the way a batter reached base is written outside the diamond. However, some people prefer to write how the batter reached base in the middle of the diamond. Do whatever makes sense to you.

The Difference Between Radio and Television

Phil Rizzuto, the Hall of Fame Yankee shortstop of the 1950s, became a commentator with the Yankees after he retired. Rizzuto once said: "I like radio better than television because if you make a mistake on radio, they don't know. You can make up anything on the radio."

Other Scoring Symbols

More things happen in baseball games than just hits and outs. Here is a more thorough list of the common scoring symbols. To use these, just write the symbol in the box of the player who was out or advanced a base.

BB   Base on balls, or, you can write W for walk

K   Strikeout. If the batter struck out looking (meaning he just stood there while the umpire called a pitch over home plate for strike three), then you can write a backward K.

HBP   Hit batsman

SF   Sacrifice fly

S or SAC   Sacrifice bunt

E#   Error, followed by the number of the fielder that made the error. For example, an error by the second baseman would be written E4.

DP   Double play (including the fielder numbers involved in the play)

TP   Triple play (including the fielder numbers involved in the play). Triple plays are extremely rare, so if you score one of these, save the scorecard.

G   Ground ball. If it's not clear that the ball was hit on the ground, write a G.

L   Line drive

F   Usually means that the ball was in foul territory when it was caught. A foul pop-up to the catcher would be scored 2F.

Other symbols you might use that don't describe what the batter did but often tell you that the runners moved up can be put in a corner of the box:

SB   Stolen base

CS   Caught stealing (include the fielder numbers involved in the play)

PB   Passed ball—this is when the catcher drops a ball he should have caught, allowing a runner to advance

WP   Wild pitch—this is when a pitch is so bad that the catcher didn't have a good chance to catch it, and a runner advances.

This game goes on, and on, and on...

Extra Innings

Use the clue under the blank space to come up with a word. Write this word in the box. When you add the word "IN," the new word has a totally different meaning!

1. _____ I N = to start
   (to plead for money)

2. _____ I N = small house in the woods
   (taxi)

3. _____ I N = springtime bird with
   (steal)   red breast

4. _____ I N = heavy, shiny fabric
   (past tense of sit)

5. _____ I N = penguin-like bird with
   (short breath out)   colorful beak

Dropped Third Strikes

When first base is open or when there are two outs, the catcher must hold on to the third strike. If the ball hits the ground before he catches it, he must get the out by tagging the batter or throwing to first base. Usually, the catcher does this without trouble. However, if the third strike was a wild pitch, or if the catcher makes a bad throw to first, the runner could be safe, but the pitcher still gets statistical credit for a strikeout. If this happens, on your scorecard you would write K-E2 (if the catcher made a bad throw) or K-WP (if the pitcher made a wild pitch).

The First Scorecard

The first scorecard was created by the Knickerbocker ball club way back in 1845.

Baseball Scoring Questions and Answers

Here are some frequently asked questions about scorekeeping.

How Do You Decide Who Is the Winning Pitcher?

Every game has a winning and losing pitcher. The winning pitcher is the one who was pitching for the winning team at the time they took the lead and did not lose the lead again.

For example, Jon Lester starts a game for the Red Sox against the Indians. The Red Sox take a 4-0 lead in the early innings and go on to win the game 4-3. Lester becomes the winning pitcher since his team never gave up the lead.

However, this game is different: The Red Sox take their 4-0 lead, but the Indians come back and tie the game. The Red Sox bring in a relief pitcher in the seventh inning and then score two runs in the eighth and win 6-4. The relief pitcher gets the win because he was the pitcher when his team took the lead and didn't lose it again.

Starting pitchers get more wins because they pitch more innings. A starting pitcher is required to pitch at least five innings to earn a win, but a reliever can earn a win no matter how few batters he faces.

Losing pitchers are determined in the opposite way. If a pitcher gives up the runs that put the other team ahead and his team never catches up, then he gets the loss.

What Does the Official Scorer Do?

The official scorer is someone at every game whose job is to decide how to score certain plays. When a fielder drops a

ball or throws a ball badly, the scorer will decide if it is a hit or an error. Official scorers also decide whether a pitch is a wild pitch or a passed ball, and they make other, more obscure scoring decisions. Official scorers decide only how the game is recorded statistically—they cannot overrule an umpire's call.

Why Do the Managers and Umpires Meet at Home Plate Before Every Game?

You may notice that before each game there is a short meeting between the umpires and the managers or coaches. This meeting has two purposes. The first is to exchange the lineup cards—each manager hands the umpire and the opposing manager a copy of his lineup. After the meeting, no more changes are allowed to the lineup.

The second purpose is to discuss the ground rules. Every stadium is built differently, and it's important that everyone understands the specific rules for what is considered in-play and what is foul territory. Some ballparks have a line on a high fence. If the ball is over that line it's a home run. Other stadiums have a high wall, but the rule is if it hits the wall, it's not a home run but still in play. Everything about the field needs to be talked about so there are no problems with the rules during the game. You probably do the same thing before playing any game with your friends, when you stop and go over the rules.

A Portion of a Sample Scorecard

You learned how to read the box score from Game 5 of the 2010 World Series between the Giants and the Rangers. Later in this chapter, you'll see the Giants' half of a scorecard from that game. (The Rangers' half would be on the other side.)

The Magic Number

Near the end of the baseball season teams start to figure out the "magic number." This is how many games the leading team must win, and how many games any other team must lose, for the leader to win the pennant (championship in their league).

There's some tricky math here. Pretend you have two teams—Team A and Team X. Team A is the leading team in the league, having won the most games so far. Team X is any other team in the league.

Follow the steps below using the scores from our sample teams. You can use the same steps with your favorite teams!

The season has 162 scheduled games.

	won	lost
TEAM A	93	59
TEAM X	89	63

games played so far: 152

Games TEAM X has won _____

ADD games TEAM X has left _____

SUBTRACT games TEAM A has won _____

ADD the number 1 _____

THE MAGIC NUMBER _____

Keeping Score

Most of this game was pretty easy to score. For example, look at the fourth inning: Posey grounded out to the third baseman, Ross struck out swinging, and Uribe flied out to center. The pitcher for the Rangers (Cliff Lee) seemed to be dominant—you don't see anyone getting past first base until the seventh inning.

The seventh inning of this scorecard was the most exciting. Go through it batter by batter to find out what happened. Ross hit a single. Uribe also hit a single, and Ross went to second base. Huff put down a sacrifice bunt, the pitcher threw him out, and the runners moved to second and third with one out. Burrell struck out, and the pitcher had a good chance to get out of the inning without giving up any runs. But Rentería hit a three-run homer. His runs batted in are noted by his name. This home run made the difference in the game; the Giants won, 3-1, to take the World Series title. Since this inning had so much going on and was so exciting, you might choose to make a few notes about it at the bottom of the scorecard page.

Now, if you're a Giants fan, you might ask Edgar Rentería to autograph this scorecard, then frame it and put it on the wall of your room. Of course, if you're a Rangers fan, you might just put the scorecard in your desk drawer and try to forget about it.

What about Pinch Hitters?

When a pinch hitter comes to the plate, draw a heavy vertical line before the box when he comes up. Then put his name next to the name of the player he replaced. If a new pitcher comes into the game, draw a heavy horizontal line on top of the box for the first batter he faces.

Sample Scorecard

This is how a finished scorecard might look.

2010 WORLD SERIES GAME
SAN FRANCISCO
DATE: November 1, 2010
VS: Texas

Pos.	Name		1	2	3	4	5	6	7	8	9
9	Torres		K		1			6-3		2F	
4	Sanchez		6-3		1L		1			7L	
2	Posey		1			5-3		9		5-4 / 1	
7	Ross		6			K			◆ 1	FC	
5	Uribe			K		8			◆ 1		K
3	Huff			4-3			6-4 DP E3		SAC 1-3		4-3
0	Burrell			7L			K		K		K
6	Rentería 3RBI				4		6-4-3 DP		◆ HR		
8	Rowand				7L			K	9		

What kind of baseball players practice in the Arctic Circle?

I wonder if they pitch snowballs?

Color in each box with a dot in the upper right-hand corner to find the silly answer to this riddle:

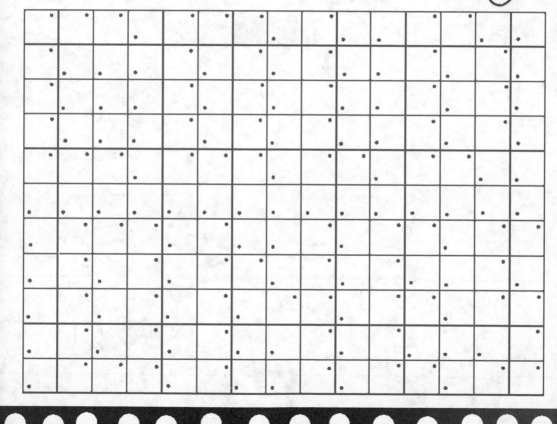

Chapter 9
Beyond the Major Leagues

Baseball fans love to go to major-league games as well as watch, read, and tell stories about their favorite teams. But you can enjoy baseball even if you're not watching the Yankees or the Red Sox. You can watch minor-league, high school, or college baseball—in fact, these teams are sometimes even more fun to follow, because you can get closer to the action and to the players. You can collect baseball cards, and play fantasy baseball. There's more to baseball than just, well, baseball!

Getting to the Majors

Everyone knows that major-league baseball players are the best in the world. But *how* do the teams know they're getting the best players? It's not like just anyone can stop by Busch Stadium and ask for a tryout! Before a player makes it to the major leagues, he's played baseball for 10–15 years. He's played in youth leagues, in high school, probably in a summer league, maybe in college, and in the minor leagues. Teams watch players at each of these levels to find out who they think they want on their major-league team.

High School Baseball

Though their games don't usually draw thousands of fans like the football games do, most every high school in the country fields a baseball team. The season usually starts in March, earlier in warm-weather areas like Florida, and finishes in late May. High school teams play about 20 games per season.

WORDS to KNOW

varsity: The varsity team is made up of a school's best players. Some schools have a junior varsity team for younger players or those who aren't quite good enough for varsity.

WORDS to KNOW

professional: A professional baseball player is paid to play; an amateur baseball player volunteers to play for a team for fun, or to improve his skills. Major leaguers are professionals, but so are players in the minor leagues. College and high school players are amateurs.

Does Anyone Skip the Minor Leagues?

Very rarely, a player is signed who is ready to play in the major leagues right away. Cincinnati pitcher Mike Leake went straight from college to the Reds in 2010. Before that, in 2000 Xavier Nady went straight from college to the Padres. Everyone else in those ten years played at least some minor-league baseball.

Becoming a Professional Baseball Player: The Draft

Major-league teams are always scouting, sending out expert watchers to find out who the best young players are. The 30 teams get competitive with each other to convince the best teenagers to play for them.

A player who was born in North America cannot choose which team to play for. First, he has to enter a draft. In June, teams take turns picking players, just like you might pick teams on the playground. A high school graduate who is picked, say, by the Mariners has three choices:

- He can sign a contract with the Mariners. In this case, he must stay with the Mariners until he's played six years in the major leagues (or until he's traded to a different team).
- He can refuse to sign a contract with the Mariners and instead wait a year to re-enter the draft to be chosen by a different team.
- He can refuse to sign with the Mariners and instead go to college. In this case, he has to play in college for three years before re-entering the draft.

A player who was not born in North America, or a player who entered the draft but wasn't drafted by anyone, can choose to sign a contract with any team. Once he signs a contract, he belongs to that team until he's played six years in the majors.

The Minor Leagues

A player who signs an initial contract with a major-league team probably isn't ready to play for that team yet. Pretty much everyone starts his career in the minor leagues.

Minor-league teams play in smaller towns with smaller stadiums than major-league teams. They travel short distances to play their away games, but they travel by bus, not the fancy private jets that major-league teams get.

Each major-league team supports a bunch of minor-league teams at different levels. Drafted players usually start at the lowest levels, called "Rookie League" and "Class A." The best players at each level get to move up a level after a year or so. The top minor-league level is called "AAA," or "triple-A." The best players on a team's AAA team can be called up to the majors.

the Show: Some college players, and all minor leaguers, are trying to make baseball their career. They say their goal is to make it to the Show, which is slang for the major leagues.

College Baseball

Most sports fans have watched college football and college basketball. College baseball can be just as exciting, especially in June during the College World Series.

College baseball teams are made up of students, though many of these students have scholarships that pay for them to go to school. They play about 60 games each year, starting around March and finishing in May.

After the end of the regular season, 64 teams are chosen for the NCAA tournament. They are divided into groups of four teams, which each play a double-elimination tournament over a weekend in early June. These first-round games are called the "regionals."

The winners of the regionals are paired the next weekend for the "superregionals." Whichever team is the first to win two games in the superregionals gets to go to the College World Series.

The College World Series is held in Omaha, Nebraska, every year. The eight teams who won their superregionals play two double-elimination tournaments. The winners of

NCAA: Baseball—and other sports, too—is an important part of college life. NCAA stands for the National Collegiate Athletic Association. The NCAA was founded in 1906 primarily to govern football, but now this organization runs all sports played by its member schools.

How Does a Double-Elimination Tournament Work?

"Double-elimination" means that a team plays until they lose twice. Four teams start the tournament by playing a game. The next day, the teams that won play against each other, and the teams that lost play each other. After the second day, one team will have lost twice—they're out. Two teams will have lost only once; they play each other, and the loser is out. The two remaining teams play each other until one of those teams has two losses. The team that's left is the winner.

each of these mini-tournaments play each other in a best-of-three series for the National Championship.

All of the CWS games are played at the same stadium in Omaha. The teams and their fans take over the city for two weeks in June, using up all of the space in the local hotels. One special part of the CWS is the friendliness that develops among fans of all the teams. Since there are games every day in the same place, and since it's summertime when schools are out, the fans can get to know each other as part of a baseball vacation.

Baseball Cards

Baseball cards are the size of playing cards. They have a picture of a player on one side; the other side lists his career stats and a short description of his career highlights. Your card collection is a reflection of your favorite teams and your favorite players, but as you get older your collection can help you remember past seasons.

Acquiring Baseball Cards

You can buy baseball cards in lots of different places, like department stores or online sellers, specialist card stores, dealers, and sellers on eBay might have rare or especially interesting cards.

Cards come in packs of several cards. Many companies make baseball cards, each with a different look. Topps, Panini America (formerly Donruss), and Upper Deck are among the most popular card-making companies. Most packs include a random assortment of current players—the fun is seeing which players you get when you open the pack. New cards come out every season, as they have since the early 1900s.

Most card buyers enjoy collecting the cards for the fun of it. The cards themselves have a glossy look and the photos are sometimes really cool action shots from a game. The statistics on the back of the cards give you all sorts of information about how the player has done in his career. Reading your cards can teach you a lot about your favorite players, so the next time you see them in a game, you have a better appreciation for who they are and where they've come from.

There are more serious collectors who buy and sell older or special cards for lots of money. But baseball card collecting is not about monetary value—it's about savoring the game of baseball.

WORDS to KNOW

commons: Commons are cards of average players, not superstars. These cards aren't usually valuable to professional collectors, but they might still have value to you if the player is one of your favorites or if he plays for your favorite team.

Dugout

One letter has been dug out of each of the following common baseball words. Fill in the missing letters. Then, transfer those letters to the corresponding boxes in the grid to form the answer to this riddle:

What's another nickname for a baseball bat?

1. U N I _ O R M
2. G _ O V E
3. P L A _ O F F
4. _ L I D E
5. S _ I N G

6. F _ N
7. B U N _
8. C A _ C H E R
9. S T _ A L
10. _ U N

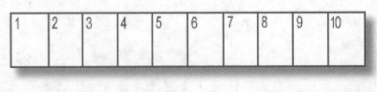

1	2	3	4	5	6	7	8	9	10

Collectible Cards

Sometimes the most valuable cards are those that accidentally get printed with a few mistakes or differences. Can you find the nine differences between these two cards?

Collectible Words

See if you can collect nine words hiding in the word **COLLECTIBLE**.

Extra Fun: Try to have all nine words use only four letters.

Some Baseball Card History

Professional baseball began at the end of the 1860s, and the first baseball cards were printed by the late 1880s. These early cards were printed on the cardboard backs of cigarette packs. Top players of the day like Cap Anson and Buck Ewing were among the first players to appear on cards. Pretty soon, in the early 1900s, a number of cigarette manufacturers were printing cards of the best players, such as Ty Cobb and Honus Wagner. There were far fewer copies of each card printed than there are of cards today.

By the 1930s chewing gum companies were also making baseball cards, and collecting these cards was becoming more popular. In 1933 the Goudey Chewing Gum Company accidentally forgot to print card number 106 in their set, a card of All-Star (and future Hall-of-Famer) Napoleon Lajoie. So many collectors sent letters asking for the missing card that the company had to print more in 1934, and it sent them to the people who had written in. This was one of the first indications that card collecting was becoming popular.

Then, in 1952, Topps made its first baseball cards with statistics of the players on the back. Card collecting was very popular through the 1960s and 1970s, but it wasn't until the late 1980s that rich collectors began to pay high prices for old cards. Some people began to see baseball cards as an investment, like putting money in the stock market. Today, card collecting isn't quite as popular as it was at the start of the 1990s, but many, many fans still savor their collections.

Stick of Gum

Once upon a time, one of the things you would always find in a pack of baseball cards was a long, pink stick of chewing gum. This isn't very common anymore, but it was standard for many years.

FUN FACT

The Most Expensive Card Ever

Pirates shortstop Honus Wagner did not want his card associated with cigarettes, so he asked that the tobacco company stop printing his cards. Therefore, only a few cards of this legendary player exist. His 1909 card, known to collectors as T-206, is now so rare that at an auction in New York City it sold for $640,000.

What Should You Do with Your Baseball Cards?

The easy answer to that question is—anything you want, especially anything that makes collecting cards fun. Here are some ideas of ways to enjoy your collection.

- **Read your cards.** You may think you know everything about your favorite player, but you might be surprised by some new information on that player's card. You might learn something about a player that makes you like him more—for example, he may have grown up in your hometown, or he may have gone to your favorite college.

- **Trade with your friends.** If you are buying lots of packs of cards, you will end up with several copies of the same player's card. Offer to give a duplicate to a friend if your friend will give you a card that you really want. Or, say you're trying to collect the whole starting lineup for your favorite team. You might be able to fill in the cards you don't have by trading.

- **Use cards as decorations.** Is the wall behind your desk or over your bed bare? Does your locker need something on the door? Use baseball cards to decorate. You could change the players you have on display every month or every year based on how the players do.

- **Get autographs.** If you know that you might have a chance to get a player's autograph—say, you have front-row tickets to a game, or you're going to hear a player speak—bring that player's card and ask him to sign it.

Fantasy Baseball

Have you ever wanted to own a baseball team? If so, you should start saving your money now—it costs close to $1 billion to buy a major-league team. But you and your friends can run your own fantasy baseball teams this season without paying any money at all.

In fantasy baseball, you choose major-league players to be on your team. The better your players perform, the better your team does. Since you're in charge of your team, you can make trades, bench players who aren't doing well, set starting lineups, put players on the disabled list—pretty much everything a real baseball owner does.

How Fantasy Baseball Works

Fantasy baseball teams are ranked based on statistics. Usually a league keeps track of ten categories. Your team gets credit for the statistics of all players in your starting lineup. If one of your players hits a home run, your team gets a home run. If one of your pitchers strikes out eight batters, your team adds eight strikeouts to its total.

In head-to-head fantasy leagues, you play a "game" against another team in your league each week. You have to do better than your opponent in each category. For example, if your pitchers record five saves this week and your opponent's pitchers only record four saves, then you win the "saves" category. If you win more categories than your opponent, then you win the game! Whichever team wins the most games by the end of the year is the champion.

In rotisserie leagues, you add up your statistics for the whole season. You get points for every team you beat in each category. Whoever gets the most points at the end of the season is the league champion.

Which Stats Does Your League Use?

Leagues usually keep track of ten statistics. For offensive players, your team earns points for batting average, home runs, runs batted in, stolen bases, and runs. Pitchers earn points for wins, saves, strikeouts, earned run average, and base runners per inning. But you can find (or create) a league that keeps track of pretty much any stats.

Scoring a Rotisserie League

Let's say you're playing in a six-team league. The best team in each category would earn six points; the second-best team, five points; and so on. Consider the "batting average" category:

Batting Averages

Team Name	average	points
Electric Marshmallows	.310	6
Varied Buntings	.303	5
Water Foul	.302	4
Screaming Boiled Lobsters	.296	3
Area 51 Greenmen	.280	2
Frumious Bandersnachi	.278	1

The nine other categories are scored the same way. Then, you add up each team's total points in all categories to see who wins.

Determining Who's on Your Team

All fantasy baseball owners want Miguel Cabrera on their team. But he can only be on one team in each league. So how do you decide who gets which players? There are two common methods: the draft and the auction. The draft is simpler and is the best way to go if you're new to fantasy baseball. Advanced players can try out an auction.

In a fantasy baseball draft, teams take turns selecting players. On your turn, you can choose any player who hasn't already been chosen. But you have to be sure to fill every position on your team!

In an auction, each team is given a budget of pretend money, say, $100. A player is mentioned, then each team can bid for that player. Whoever bids the most money gets the player. But you only have that $100 for your whole team. If you spend too much on one player, you'll be stuck without money to fill out your roster.

After the draft or auction, you still have to manage your team. If one of your players gets hurt or isn't doing well, you'll need to replace him. The easiest way to obtain players is through "waivers." Players who aren't on a team are listed on the "waiver wire." You can choose a player from this list to be on your team. Each league makes rules about how often you can pick up one of these players, and about what happens if two teams want the same player.

Another option for improving your team is to make trades. If your team has plenty of one statistic but needs to do better in another, you might consider a trade. For example, your team might have a whole lot of saves, but not very many stolen bases. So, you could offer to give another team one of your closers, like Mariano Rivera, in exchange for someone who steals a lot of bases, like Jose Reyes.

Fantasy Baseball Strategy

The fantasy team owners who do the best are the ones who pay careful attention to the players. Sure, you want to pick star players, the guys everyone knows about. But pretty soon after your draft starts, there won't be any stars left. So how do you know which players to pick?

Before your draft, you should read about every team. Find out what new players are on the team. Know who is likely to start at each position. Then, make a list of who you think are the best ten or fifteen major-league players at each position, and a list of the 30 or so players you absolutely want if you can have them.

After the draft, it's usually a good idea to leave your team alone for a few weeks to see how your players do. Be careful—in the excitement of the early season, it's tempting to give up on a good player who starts with a slump; you might want to pick up a poorer player who happens to be off to a hot start. More often than not, though, you'll do best by sticking with your players who have a history of producing strong stats. But if one of your players is injured, or if he starts losing playing time—then it might be time to make a move.

Who Keeps Track of Your League?

Years ago, people who played fantasy baseball had to keep careful track of their team by reading newspaper box scores every day and writing down each player's stats. Nowadays, though, the Internet makes keeping track of your team's stats simple. Some Internet fantasy baseball services are free, like those at *www.yahoo.com* or *www.cbssports.com*. For your first season of fantasy baseball, a free service will work fine—your parents can easily help you sign up with one of these.

WHIP: WHIP stands for Walks plus Hits per Inning Pitched. Many leagues keep track of this category, which means almost the same thing as base runners per inning. Only the very best pitchers' WHIPs are below 1.000. A good WHIP is 1.100 or 1.150.

Flash in the Pan

In 2006, Chris Shelton of the Tigers hit nine home runs in just the first two weeks of the season! Some fantasy owners rushed to pick him up . . . but he hit only seven more homers all year. Oops!

Other websites require a registration fee to play. These sites will usually provide more options in terms of the stats your league can use, and you'll usually get more detailed (maybe even live) scoring updates, message boards, and "expert" advice. But you don't need to pay to play fantasy baseball unless you're an advanced enough player to really want these extra features.

The neatest thing about fantasy baseball is how much you learn about major-league players. Fantasy leagues also give you baseball topics to talk to your friends about. Try owning a team for a season—your fantasy experience will probably allow you to appreciate the real game of baseball even more.

FUN FACT

Public Leagues

If you can't find enough friends to make a fantasy league, try joining a "public league" on a fantasy baseball website. You will be matched with other players of similar experience.

Name Game

This baseball card collector has gotten some pretty famous autographs. Unfortunately, the players signed their names too big! Can you tell who signed each card? Choose names from the list.

Barry Bonds
Willie Mays
Nolan Ryan
Pete Rose
Alex Rodriguez
Cy Young
Sandy Koufax
Ty Cobb
Jimmie Foxx
Tom Seaver
Greg Maddux
Lou Gehrig
Hank Aaron

assist

When a player makes a throw of any kind to get an out, whether it's an infielder throwing a batter out running to first base or an outfielder throwing a runner out at home plate, the player gets an assist.

backstop

The fence behind home plate is the backstop. In parks and on Little League fields, the backstop is usually a high fence that slants over home plate so that foul balls don't fly off and hurt people passing by. (Backstop is also a slang term used for a catcher.)

battery

A term for the pitcher and catcher. If, for example, Joe Nathan is pitching and Joe Mauer is catching, they are the battery in that game.

batting order

The order in which players on a team come up and take their turn as the hitter. The manager or coach of the team decides the batting order before the game and lists the players, first through ninth, in order of when they will hit. If a batter bats out of turn, he can be called out.

bleachers

The seats behind the outfield wall are called the bleachers. Sometimes, like in Wrigley Field, the fans who sit there call themselves the "bleacher bums."

blooper

A ball that is not hit very hard but sort of pops over the infielders and lands in front of the outfielders for a hit.

box score

A grid containing a summary of the game statistics, including how each player did.

bullpen

Where the relief pitchers warm up before coming in to pitch. Most stadiums have bullpens beyond the outfield fences, while some have them in foul territory.

bunt

To bunt is to hold the bat horizontally, one hand on the handle and the other way up on the bat (don't hold it with your hand around the front of the bat, just pinch it from the back part so your finger doesn't get squished by the pitch). The idea is to let the ball just bounce off the bat and stay fair so the runners can move up a base, which is known as a "sacrifice." You can also bunt for a hit by pushing the bat so that the ball rolls a little farther toward third base or first base.

cleanup hitter

The cleanup hitter is the fourth hitter in the lineup.

closer

The relief pitcher that comes in to get the final outs and the save is the team's closer.

commentators

The broadcasters or announcers who are at the ballpark describing what is going on in the game on either television or radio.

commons

Baseball cards of average players, not superstars. These cards aren't usually valuable to professional collectors but they still might have value to you or to a friend if the player is one of your favorites, or if that player is on your favorite team.

Glossary

contact hitter
A hitter that makes contact with the ball often and doesn't strike out very much.

count
The number of balls and strikes that have been pitched to the hitter. For example, two balls and two strikes would be a "two and two" count.

dinger
A slang term for a home run.

disabled list
When a player is injured the team may put the player on what is called the disabled list, or DL. This means the player cannot play for 15 or more days and the team can call someone else up from the minor leagues to put on their roster of active players.

double
A hit that gets the batter safely to second base.

double play
When two players get called out after one player hits the ball.

error
When a fielder drops or bobbles a ball or throws it so the other fielder can't catch it and it results in the batter or runner being safe, it's called an error on the fielder.

extra innings
If a game is tied after the regulation nine innings, teams go into extra innings, which means they play additional innings until someone scores the winning run or runs. The home team always gets the last turn at bat.

fan
Besides being one of the people rooting for your favorite team, to fan in baseball is another term for striking out.

foul ball
A ball that is hit that is not in fair territory. Foul balls count as strike one and strike two, but not as strike three unless you're bunting. In the big leagues, many foul balls go into the stands and are souvenirs to the fans who catch them.

foul line
The lines extending from home plate past first and third base all the way to the outfield fence that separate fair territory from foul territory. A fly ball that lands on the foul line is fair.

foul out
When a ball is hit in the air in foul territory and caught by an opposing player for an out.

foul pole
A ball that flies over the outfield fence is only a home run if it leaves the field in fair territory. The foul poles make it easy to tell whether a ball is a home run: One side of the pole is fair, the other is foul. But if the ball hits the foul pole, it's a home run.

foul territory
The part of the playing field that is outside of the foul lines and not part of the actual field of play.

full count
Three balls and two strikes is considered a full count—one more ball is a walk and one more strike is a strikeout.

grand slam

A grand slam is when you hit a home run with the bases loaded (a player on each base). The most runs you can score on one hit are on a grand slam!

head-to-head

A type of fantasy league in which your team's stats are compared to one other team's stats on a week-by-week basis.

hit and run

A hit-and-run play is where the base runners start running as the pitcher pitches the ball and the batter swings. This play helps avoid a double play and can also get runners to advance more bases on a base hit.

hits

A player gets a hit when he or she hits the ball and then runs to the base without making an out. Here are the different kinds of hits you can get: single, double, triple, and home run.

home run

You touch all the bases including home plate (where you start from as the batter). If you hit one over the fence, it's a home run and you should be very happy!

home team

The team most of the local fans root for since they are the team hosting the game on their field. The home team always bats second in the inning, called the bottom of the inning.

inning

An inning is a period of play in which each team has a turn at bat. Each team gets three outs. A regulation major-league game lasts nine innings.

inside-the-park home run

Most home runs go over the outfield fence, but a fast runner might be able to get all the way around the bases on a ball that stays in the ballpark on an inside-the-park homer—it's very rare!

intentional walk

An intentional walk is when a pitcher walks a batter on purpose. Sometimes this makes it easier to get a double play if there are other runners on second and/or third. Sometimes a batter is walked intentionally because the player is very good and the pitcher doesn't want to give up a home run.

left on base

You may see this in the box score (lob) or hear broadcasters mention it. This indicates how many players were left standing on the bases when the final out was made to end an inning.

mound

The mound, or pitching mound, is the dirt circle in the middle of the infield diamond where the pitcher stands. It's called a mound because the pitcher stands almost a foot higher than the rest of the infield.

on deck

The batter who is scheduled to hit next is considered to be waiting on deck. Usually there is an on-deck circle where the player stands and takes practice swings.

opposite field

When the announcer says a hitter got a hit to the opposite field, it means the ball went the opposite way from where it should go for that type of hitter.

When the bat is swung around, most left-handed hitters will hit the ball to right field, and right-handed hitters will hit the ball to left field. If the hitter hits it to the other field, a right-handed hitter hitting to right field and vice versa, it's called hitting to the opposite field.

overrun

This is when you are going too fast and run over the base. You're allowed to overrun first base, but if you overrun second or third, you can be tagged out.

pennant

The team that wins the National League or American League Championship is said to have won the pennant—then they play in the World Series.

pickoff

If there's a base runner and the pitcher throws to the fielder, who catches the runner off base and tags that runner for an out, it's called a pickoff.

pinch hitter

A hitter who bats in place of someone else.

pinch runner

A pinch runner is a player who comes in to run for someone else. This may be a faster runner who can steal a base or score a run more easily.

prospect

A player who is thought to have skills that will make that player a future star is considered to be a prospect.

putout

Whenever a fielder catches a ball that results in an out, it's a putout. This includes a first baseman taking a throw from an infielder and stepping on the base, or a catcher on a strikeout.

rain delay

A rain delay is when the game is stopped because of rain, but they hope to continue and finish it later. The umpires decide when to stop, restart, or call a game (cancel it) because of rain.

rain out

A rain out is when a game is called off because of rain. If this happens before the fifth inning, the game doesn't count. If it's after the fifth inning it's considered an official game, and whichever team was ahead at the time wins.

reliever

A reliever or relief pitcher is the pitcher who comes in to replace the starting pitcher.

rookie

A first-year player is known as a rookie.

roster

A roster is the listing of players on the team. Major-league rosters include 25 players for most of the season.

rotisserie

A type of fantasy baseball league in which your team's stats are compared to other team's stats for the whole year.

run

A run in baseball is scored whenever a player comes all the way around the bases and crosses home plate. The team who scores the most runs wins.

rundown play

When a runner is trapped between bases, the fielders play what looks like a game of monkey-in-the-middle as they throw the ball back and forth trying to tag the runner and not let him or her get to the next base. Usually a runner will be tagged out in a rundown play unless one of the fielders misses the ball.

single

You get to first base safely without anyone catching the ball in the air, tagging you out, or throwing to first base before you get there.

save

When a pitcher comes into a close ballgame and gets the final outs it is called a save.

scoring position

When a runner is on second or third base, he is considered in scoring position, meaning it's easier to score on a hit.

signs

Some people hold up signs in the stands, but in baseball there are other signs. The catcher puts down fingers to give the pitcher a sign as to what pitch to throw. There are also signs relayed from the coach at third base to the batter. Coaches are usually busy touching their cap, tugging on their ear, and doing all sorts of movements. They are signaling the batter to take a pitch, swing away, bunt, or perhaps hit and run. They are also often signaling runners on base. Next time you're at a game, watch the third-base coach for a minute and see what he's up to. If you're playing, always check what the sign from the coach is before the pitcher pitches.

slide

A slide is when a runner dives feet first or head first into a base. Be careful if you try sliding—ask your coach to help you learn how to slide properly so you don't get hurt.

southpaw

A left-handed pitcher is sometimes referred to as a southpaw.

spitball or spitter

Once upon a time, in the early years of baseball, it used to be okay for pitchers to spit on the ball before throwing it. It made the ball make some strange movements, and batters had a hard time hitting it. The rules no longer allow this pitch to be thrown.

starter

The starter is the pitcher that begins pitching the game for the team.

take

To take a pitch means to not swing at it. If a pitcher is having trouble throwing strikes, a batter may take a pitch to see if the pitcher can throw it in the strike zone. If the batter has three balls and no strikes, it's a good idea to take the pitch to try and get a walk.

tarp

The tarp is what the grounds crew covers the field with while the teams, umpires, and fans wait for the rain to stop so they can continue the game. The tarp is a giant piece of plastic that usually covers just the infield.

triple
A hit that gets the batter safely to third base.

triple play
A triple play is a very rare play where one player hits the ball and all three outs are made. Naturally, there has to be no one out and at least two runners on base for a triple play.

umpire
An umpire is the person who is refereeing the game or ruling on the plays in the game. The umpire rules whether a pitch is a strike or a ball, if a ball that is hit is fair or foul, or if a batter or runner is safe or out.

visiting team
The team that comes to play on another team's field. The visiting team always bats first in the inning, known as the top of the inning.

walk-off home run
This refers to a home run in the bottom of the ninth or in the home team's at bat in the bottom of an extra inning that wins and ends the game. Following the home run, the teams walk off the field—hence the name.

WHIP
Walks plus hits per inning pitched is an important statistical category for fantasy baseball. Anything below 1.2 is pretty good.

wild card
In major-league baseball there are three divisions in each league, but four teams make the playoffs each year. The fourth team, the wild card team, is the best second-place team from any one of the three divisions.

Appendix B
Books, Magazines, Websites, and More

Baseball Books

Historical Baseball Books

The Sporting News Selects: Baseball's 25 Greatest Moments by Ron Smith and Joe Morgan

The All-Century Team by Mark Vancil looks at the 100 best players of the 20th century.

The Story of Negro League Baseball by William Brashler has the history and the stars of these leagues.

300 Great Baseball Cards of the 20th Century is a historical look at baseball cards from Beckett Publishing.

The Echoing Green: The Untold Story of Bobby Thomson, Ralph Branca, and the Shot Heard Round the World by Joshua Prager gives details about how the Giants stole catchers' signs from their center field clubhouse, leading to Thomson's famous home run.

How to Play the Game

Jeff Burroughs' Little League Instructional Guide

Baseball Just for Kids: Skills, Strategies and Stories to Make You a Better Ballplayer by Jerry Kasoff

Touching All the Bases: Baseball for Kids of All Ages by Claire MacKay

The Art of Pitching by Tom Seaver

The Art of Hitting by Tony Gwynn

The Science of Hitting by Ted Williams

Biographies

Jackie and Me (about Jackie Robinson), *Babe and Me*, and *Honus and Me* (about Honus Wagner) by Dan Gutman, from his Baseball Card Adventure series

Lou Gehrig, Pride of the Yankees by Keith Brandt

Babe Ruth, Home Run Hero by Keith Brandt

I Had a Hammer: The Hank Aaron Story by Lonnie Wheeler with Hank Aaron himself

Lists, Quotes, Jokes, and Statistics

The Yogi Book: I Really Didn't Say Everything I Said by Yogi Berra has a lot of the funniest sayings by one funny former catcher.

Total Baseball: The Official Encyclopedia of Major League Baseball by John Thorn is loaded with statistics and very heavy.

Baseball Prospectus: The Essential Guide to the Baseball Season is a yearly guide that includes comprehensive statistics and analysis. It's a great tool to help prepare for a fantasy baseball season.

Batter Up! Baseball Activities for Kids of All Ages by Ouisie Shapiro includes a lot of fun facts, quizzes, and games. If you like the puzzles in the book you're reading now, check out *Batter Up!*

Baseball Math: Grandslam Activities and Projects for Grades 4–8 by Christopher Jennison will help you work on your math skills while having some fun.

Baseball Movies

The Pride of the Yankees, 1942, the story of Lou Gehrig

The Babe Ruth Story, 1948

The Jackie Robinson Story, 1950

Angels in the Outfield, 1951, the original

Damn Yankees, 1958, a broadway musical brought to film

The Bad News Bears, 1976

The Natural, 1984

Eight Men Out, 1988, about the 1919 Black Sox scandal

Field of Dreams, 1989

Major League, 1989

A League of Their Own, 1992, about the women's leagues of the 1940s

Angels in the Outfield, 1994, the remake

42, 2013, about Jackie Robinson

Magazines

Baseball America
This is a biweekly magazine that covers professional, college, and high school baseball, with an emphasis on the amateur draft, scouting, and minor-league development.
www.BaseballAmerica.com

Baseball Digest
This is a bimonthly magazine with stories about pro players past and present, rosters, a quiz (it's not easy), a crossword puzzle, and plenty of fun facts about the game.
www.baseballdigest.com

Baseball Weekly
Baseball Weekly is a magazine devoted to the latest info on the major leagues and even the minor leagues. Plenty of statistics and recent box scores are included in *Baseball Weekly*.

Junior Baseball
Junior Baseball is all about baseball leagues for players 7 to 17.
www.juniorbaseball.com

Sports Illustrated for Kids
Sports Illustrated for Kids has info on many sports, including baseball. The magazine includes tips on playing the game and interviews with your favorite players.
www.sikids.com

USA Today
USA Today has a great sports section with a lot about baseball, including daily reports on each team so you can see what your favorite team is up to.
www.usatoday.com

Websites

Baseball Almanac
This is a compilation of awards, records, statistics, quotes, feats, and facts in baseball history.
www.baseball-almanac.com

Baseball Reference
Up-to-date major- and minor-league statistics for each player, team, and league in baseball history.
www.baseball-reference.com

MLB.com
This is the major leagues' official baseball website. You can find anything you need there, including up-to-the-inning scores, pitching match-ups for the next several days, injury reports, trades, news, player statistics, and info on everything from spring training through the World Series. There is a history section with links to all sorts of baseball records and much, much more. In May and June you can even vote for the players for the All-Star Game.
www.mlb.com

Negro Leagues Baseball
This is a very informative site about the Negro Leagues. The history, players, and teams are all part of this interesting site. New books are featured, as are several articles that offer insight into an important part of baseball and American history.
www.negroleaguebaseball.com

Sporting News
Formerly a weekly newspaper known as the "Bible of Baseball," the website offers detailed reports and opinions about your favorite teams, as well as extensive interviews, statistics, and fantasy leagues.
www.sportingnews.com

Appendix C
Puzzle Answers

page 15 • Why do hitters . . .

Because there are more

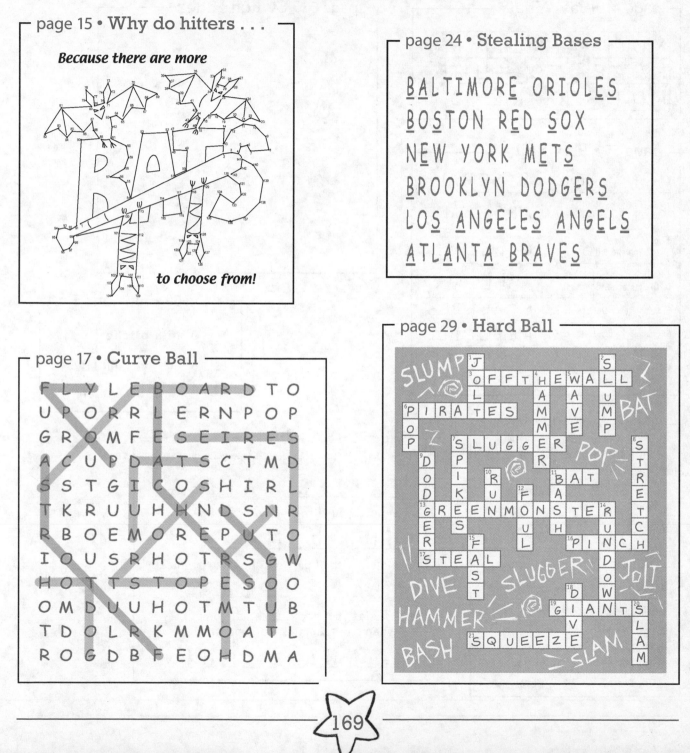

to choose from!

page 24 • Stealing Bases

BALTIMORE ORIOLES
BOSTON RED SOX
NEW YORK METS
BROOKLYN DODGERS
LOS ANGELES ANGELS
ATLANTA BRAVES

page 17 • Curve Ball

F L Y L E B O A R D T O
U P O R R L E R N P O P
G R O M F E S E I R E S
A C U P D A T S C T M D
S S T G I C O S H I R L
T K R U U H H N D S N R
R B O E M O R E P U T O
I O U S R H O T R S G W
H O T T S T O P E S O O
O M D U U H O T M T U B
T D O L R K M M O A T L
R O G D B F E O H D M A

page 29 • Hard Ball

page 41 • Say What?

Y	O	G	I	,	I		C	A	M	E
H	E	R	E		T	O		H	I	T	,
N	O	T		T	O		R	E	A	D	!

page 55 • Play Ball

1. Print the word BASEBALL.	BASEBALL
2. Switch the position of the first two letters.	ABSEBALL
3. Move the 5th letter between the 2nd and 3rd letters.	ABBSEBALL
4. Switch the positions of the 4th and 8th letters.	ABBLEALS
5. Change the 6th letter to P.	ABBLEPLS
6. Change the last letter to E.	ABBLEPLE
7. Change both B's to P's.	APPLEPLE
8. Change the 7th letter to I.	APPLEPIE

page 63 • Switch Hitter

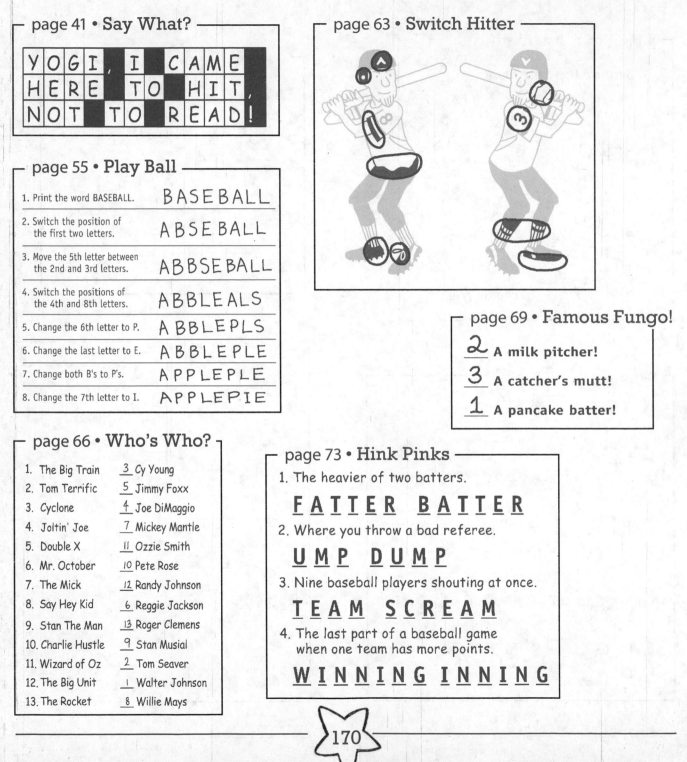

page 69 • Famous Fungo!

2 A milk pitcher!
3 A catcher's mutt!
1 A pancake batter!

page 66 • Who's Who?

1. The Big Train	3 Cy Young
2. Tom Terrific	5 Jimmy Foxx
3. Cyclone	4 Joe DiMaggio
4. Joltin' Joe	7 Mickey Mantle
5. Double X	11 Ozzie Smith
6. Mr. October	10 Pete Rose
7. The Mick	12 Randy Johnson
8. Say Hey Kid	6 Reggie Jackson
9. Stan The Man	13 Roger Clemens
10. Charlie Hustle	9 Stan Musial
11. Wizard of Oz	2 Tom Seaver
12. The Big Unit	1 Walter Johnson
13. The Rocket	8 Willie Mays

page 73 • Hink Pinks

1. The heavier of two batters.

FATTER BATTER

2. Where you throw a bad referee.

UMP DUMP

3. Nine baseball players shouting at once.

TEAM SCREAM

4. The last part of a baseball game when one team has more points.

WINNING INNING

page 78 • Baseball Diamond

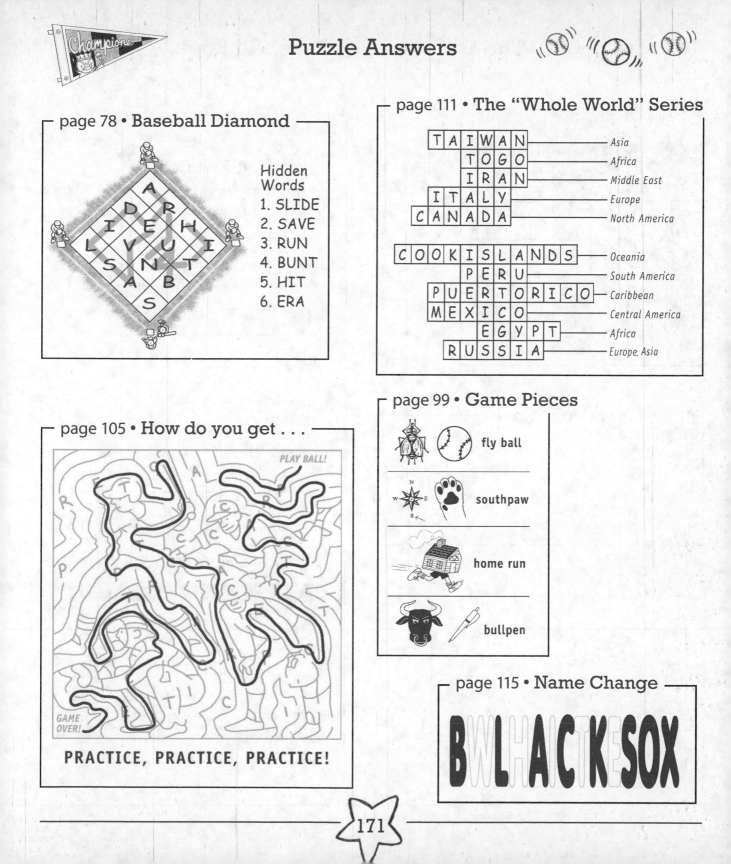

Hidden
Words
1. SLIDE
2. SAVE
3. RUN
4. BUNT
5. HIT
6. ERA

page 111 • The "Whole World" Series

T	A	I	W	A	N				— Asia
	T	O	G	O					— Africa
	I	R	A	N					— Middle East
I	T	A	L	Y					— Europe
C	A	N	A	D	A				— North America

C	O	O	K	I	S	L	A	N	D	S	— Oceania
	P	E	R	U							— South America
P	U	E	R	T	O	R	I	C	O		— Caribbean
M	E	X	I	C	O						— Central America
	E	G	Y	P	T						— Africa
R	U	S	S	I	A						— Europe, Asia

page 105 • How do you get . . .

PLAY BALL!

GAME OVER!

PRACTICE, PRACTICE, PRACTICE!

page 99 • Game Pieces

fly ball

southpaw

home run

bullpen

page 115 • Name Change

BWLHACKTESOX

page 126 • Lucky Numbers

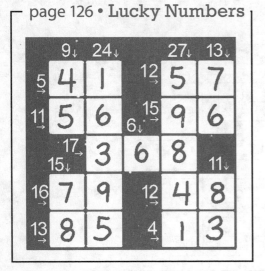

page 129 • Secret Signals

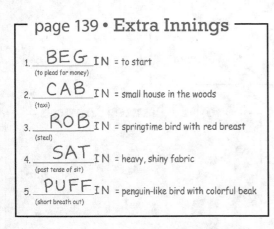

CAREFUL — THIS GUY

IS A PINCH HITTER!

page 139 • Extra Innings

1. **BEG** IN = to start
   (to plead for money)
2. **CAB** IN = small house in the woods
   (taxi)
3. **ROB** IN = springtime bird with red breast
   (steal)
4. **SAT** IN = heavy, shiny fabric
   (past tense of sit)
5. **PUFF** IN = penguin-like bird with colorful beak
   (short breath out)

page 133 • How come Drew . . .

~~AND~~	EVERY	~~CAT~~
TIME	~~GOT~~	HE
~~BAT~~	GETS	~~EAR~~
TO	~~FUR~~	THIRD
BUT	BASE	~~HIT~~
HE	~~HAT~~	GOES
~~HUT~~	HOME	~~BAG~~

page 142 • The Magic Number

The season has 162 scheduled games.

	won	lost	games played so far: 152
TEAM A	93	59	
TEAM X	89	63	

Games TEAM X has won	89
ADD games TEAM X has left	+ 10
SUBTRACT games TEAM A has won	− 93
ADD the number 1	+ 1
THE MAGIC NUMBER	= 7

page 145 • . . . Arctic Circle?

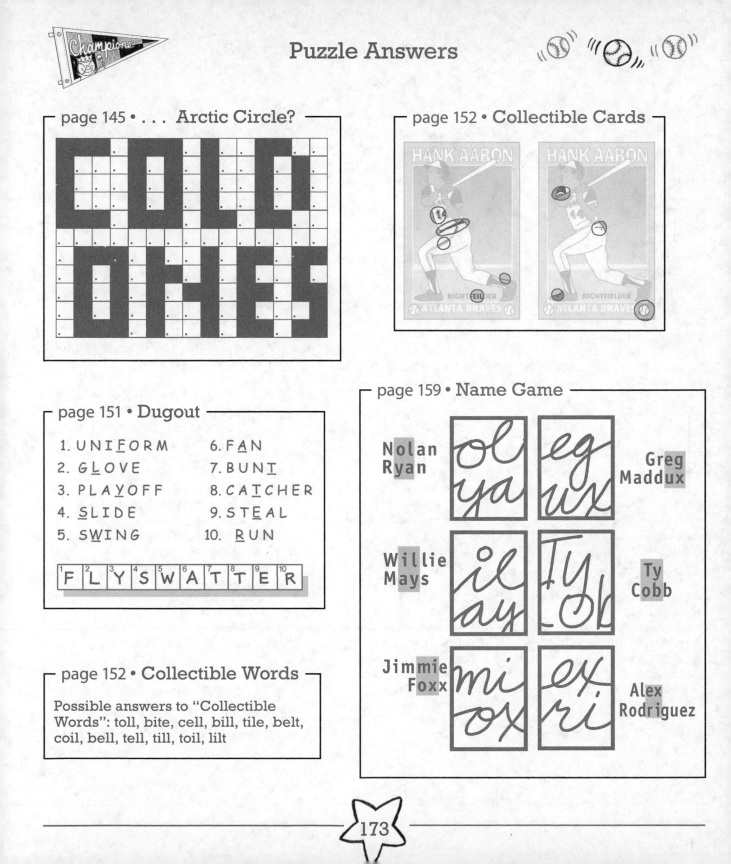

COLD ONES

page 152 • Collectible Cards

page 151 • Dugout

1. UNI F ORM
2. G L OVE
3. PLA Y OFF
4. S LIDE
5. S W ING
6. F A N
7. BUN T
8. CA T CHER
9. S T EAL
10. R U N

1	2	3	4	5	6	7	8	9	10
F	L	Y	S	W	A	T	T	E	R

page 152 • Collectible Words

Possible answers to "Collectible Words": toll, bite, cell, bill, tile, belt, coil, bell, tell, till, toil, lilt

page 159 • Name Game

Nolan Ryan — ol ya

eg ux — Greg Maddux

Willie Mays — il ay

Ty ob — Ty Cobb

Jimmie Foxx — mi ox

ex ri — Alex Rodriguez

Index